TWENTY-ONE notable Catholics are vividly portrayed by the gifted pen of Theodore Maynard in this panorama of the Catholic Church in the United States. From the earliest explorers to famous Catholics of our own century, a parade of remarkable and varied personalities passes before our eyes.

We meet dauntless heroism as St. Isaac Jogues faces torture with a prayer for his tormentors. We brave the unchartered wilderness with Bishop Flaget, Father De Smet, and Fra Junípero Serra as they bring Christ to savages who never saw a white man. We are stimulated by the fiery, brilliant, controversial Orestes Brownson. We meet outstanding ecclesiastics — Bishop Carroll, Archbishop Hughes, Cardinal Gibbons, others — watch them meet each successive challenge that has faced the Church since our nation began. We smile with the lovable Al Smith — even as we admire one of the bravest men in American public life. And we are inspired: by Mother Cabrini, our

GREAT CATHOLICS IN AMERICAN HISTORY

Great Catholics IN American History

Theodore Maynard

HANOVER HOUSE
Garden City, New York

Nihil obstat: JOHN A. GOODWINE, J. C.D.
Censor Librorum

Imprimatur: ✠ FRANCIS CARDINAL SPELLMAN
Archbishop of New York

Library of Congress Catalog Card Number 57-5792

Printed in the United States of America
First Edition

To my grandchildren

Contents

Introduction

This is an attempt to convey some idea of the development of the Catholic Church in the United States of America, not by means of the historical method—as that would require a treatment of a good many topics as well as persons—but through picturing some figures of special interest, and in many instances those associated with them, if only by way of opposition to their work. In a few instances the name that stands as the title of a chapter alone is treated; far more often, it is not. In other cases these subsidiary characters appear in several chapters, because of their impact upon many lives, even when, as in the case of Archbishop Ireland, no chapter is centered around them.

Ecclesiastical dignitaries, as such, do not often appear. Of the five bishops who are included, Bishop Healy of Portland, Maine, is the only Negro who ever occupied an American see. Another Negro (a layman) is also dealt with, and one Indian. Four laymen are presented, and four women, as well as eight religious, though only five of these can be classified as such in the strict canonical sense.

Two women who might have been included are left out, because, while American in every fibre of their being, they did most of their work abroad. One is Louise Imogen Guiney the poet, in my opinion the best that Catholic America has so far produced. The other is Mother Cornelia Connolly, who founded the Congregation of the Holy Child Jesus in England, though since her death her daughters have established several excellent schools and at least one college in the United States. I regretfully omit touching upon a life that was not merely fascinating but astonishing.

The first four people dealt with—St. Isaac Jogues, Père Marquette, Kateri Tekakwitha and Junípero Serra—were not directly concerned with the United States as we know it today. Yet who shall say that they did not greatly affect the destinies of our country? Fr. Jogues only set foot upon our soil because he, with some others, was captured upon the St. Lawrence and forcibly carried here. Fr. Marquette was primarily a missionary, yet is remembered for his exploration of the Mississippi in the interest of France, but to our subsequent advantage. Kateri Tekakwitha, though born near what is now Albany, New York, spent her last years in the region of Canada. She had no other object than perfecting her own spirituality, but her holiness makes our land more hallowed. And Fr. Serra, apart from his work of converting the Indians of California, was preserving the Pacific coast for Spain. Though Russia was hardly in a position at that time to hold a strip of over 3,000 miles, it did possess Alaska until 1867, and might well have annexed California in the late eighteenth century had it not been for Serra's foresight and vigilance.

Not until we come to John Carroll do we find an American Catholic working within the young republic. Though he was not concerned with politics, except in his unofficial attachment to the diplomatic mission sent by Congress to Canada, other members of his family were, one being a signer of the Declaration of Independence, another a signer of the Constitution. Through their work and their reputation a friendly feeling for Catholics was obtained; in particular, the religious freedom the Constitution guaranteed. Until the Revolution the Catholic Church had been absolutely proscribed in most of the British colonies, and in all of them lay under disabilities of varying strictness.

While confining myself to the present territory of the United States, I have made no attempt to give attention to every part; this is not history, but biography. I have selected those figures who happen to be of special interest to me personally, though I have also borne in mind what my readers are likely to find interesting, as well as the need of considering individuals whom everybody will admit to have had historical or social importance.

The chronological arrangement has some disadvantages, as well as conveniences. But some plan had to be adopted, and this seemed to be the best. It involves, however, a gap between the first four subjects and the rest. Under any scheme, however, there would be a similar gap, unless one started with John Carroll. Even so, I have not been rigidly consistent, for I have dealt with Alfred E. Smith last, whereas the last—if only because of the date of birth—should be Teresa Demjanovich. The shift was made because Teresa, though her cause for beatification is now being vigorously pressed, lived a short and comparatively obscure life. But Governor Smith, who long outlived her, was a man known to everybody in the United States, a candidate for the presidency and a politician of immense ability as well as of the greatest integrity.

At the end of the book will be found select bibliographies for each of the chapters. An evaluation has been attempted in the case of some of the items; more often, the bibliographical information is given without comment.

There was a temptation to give page references to books drawn upon, and also to make explanatory comments in footnotes to some matters that appear in the text, but for the sake of the average reader I have carefully refrained. If this makes no claim to be a "learned" work, it is as exactly factual as I can make it.

GREAT CATHOLICS IN AMERICAN HISTORY

I: Saint Isaac Jogues

(1607–1646)

Fortunately for all of us, the world rests upon the shoulders of commonplace men—or of men who seem to be commonplace—such as soldiers and sailors, farmers and artisans. But if Isaac Jogues does not strike one as brilliant, this may be largely due to the principle engrained in all Jesuits, that, while they should use their talents to the full, they must avoid parading them. At the same time the Jesuits admit into their order only those of respectable ability. Jogues was certainly such a man, and if he was unassuming, this was not merely because of what had been instilled into him but because he was naturally modest. It was in the most matter-of-fact way that this martyr spoke of his own sufferings; he was obviously far more concerned with doing what he could to help others who were enduring the same pangs. From the time he began his work among the Indians in Canada until his death in what is now New York, there was no day—almost no hour—when he was not in danger of a violent and exceedingly painful end, something that never ruffled his serene courage. Heroism is needed by a saint; indeed, the definition of sanctity is heroic virtue. It is therefore only fitting that this series of brief biographies should open with the story of a saint.

Isaac Jogues was born in the peaceful and prosperous city of Orleans on January 10, 1607. He was descended from a man who, after working as a laborer in a nearby market town, moved to the larger centre; there he decidedly bettered his fortunes, though without becoming rich. By the time

Isaac was born the numerous Jogueses in Orleans were all lawyers or notaries or apothecaries, and the solid and stolid complacency of such people is notorious—perhaps most of all in France. Indeed, the French have coined the word to describe them, the *bourgeoisie,* comfortable, unadventurous, and, if not actually dull in their own persons, living a life that is dull, but with which they are quite satisfied. About the last thing expected of a Jogues was that he should go out as a missionary to the Indians of New France.

That Isaac did so was due to the fortuitous circumstance that the Jesuits opened a school and college in the city. As they had long since established the reputation of being the best of educators, it was inevitable that young Jogues should be enrolled as a student; but when at about the age of seventeen he told his mother—his father had died during his student days—that he wished to enter the order, she, while sufficiently pious, felt disturbed. She would have preferred him to become a lawyer, but, if he must become a priest, what was the matter with training for the diocesan priesthood or with entering a local monastery? If he became a Jesuit, nobody could say to what distant country he might be sent. But Isaac had made up his mind, and in 1624 we find him in the Jesuit novitiate at Rouen.

The idea of going to Canada was implanted in him there by a visit at the novitiate of three missionaries who were on their way to Dieppe to take a ship for New France. When Jogues spoke to the novice master about his ambitions—up to that time he had thought of going to Constantinople as a missionary—the surprising answer came, "Brother, you will not die anywhere but in Canada." Actually, he died in what is now part of the United States, but at that time the northern part of the State of New York was a no-man's land, to which the French had perhaps a better claim than anybody else. What he said therefore sounds like a prophecy, and one actually fulfilled.

Yet the prophecy seemed to be completely falsified when the Jesuits in Canada were driven out after the British capture of Quebec. But as this had been effected by a British group acting without the slightest authority, Cardinal Richelieu insisted that Quebec be restored; this opened the door again. Meanwhile, Jogues had followed the fixed Jesuit routine: after his novitiate he had studied philosophy, then taught, and then gone on to theology. Though he did not greatly distinguish himself as a scholar, he was at least adequate. After ordination he was, in 1636, when not quite thirty, sent to New France.

It should be borne in mind as to what follows that Champlain had in 1609 made implacable enemies of the Iroquois by allying himself with the Algonquins, with whom they were perpetually at feud. To make matters worse—though it was necessary under the circumstances—the French had established fortified settlements at Three Rivers, on the northern bank of the St. Lawrence, and Montreal, an island in the river. A fort also was begun on the southern side of the great body of water. This was Fort Richelieu, almost at the mouth of the river of the same name. The Iroquois, the Five Nations —Senecas, Cayugas, Onondagas, Oneidas and Mohawks— occupied the territory between the Hudson River and the western tip of Lake Ontario. The French had blundered badly in antagonizing this powerful federation of tribes, who had the advantage of being able to procure firearms from the Dutch settlement at Fort Orange (the present Albany). The Dutch further cemented the friendship by supplying the Indians with a certain amount of fire-water. The Dutch felt they needed this alliance, for, though they loosely held the Hudson as far as Manhattan, they could not feel secure with the English colonies of New England, Pennsylvania and Virginia so close at hand, and with the French not far away.

Just what all this was to mean to him Fr. Jogues did not then know; he knew only that Iroquois war parties were to be avoided if possible. His assignment was to the Huron mission. He had often seen Algonquins and Hurons when they had come to the French settlements to sell their furs. The Hurons he could recognize from the way they wore their hair—whence came the name of *la hure,* which described the bristling ridge of hair that ran from the forehead to the nape of the neck, the rest of the head being clean shaven.

He was aware that this tribe, like the Algonquins, could be as cruel as their mortal enemies the Iroquois, for he once saw a man and a woman brought in as captives by a band of Algonquins. The two were standing upright in the canoe, singing loudly to show their disdain for the fate that awaited them. The instant the captives landed, the Algonquins on the shore—even the squaws and the children—fell upon them, biting their arms and legs like wild beasts, gnawing off a thumb, and thrusting firebrands against the naked flesh—mere preliminaries to what was to follow. One of the Jesuit priests rushed to the rescue and commanded them to stop the torture. But, though the Algonquins went no further just then, they took off the two captives to their own encampment, to torture them at leisure and then burn them alive. Yet Jogues was assured that these Indians, when among themselves, were gentle and docile and had good minds. Both on that account, and to win them from savagery, he yearned to go among them.

When at last he set out for the Huron country on Georgian Bay—an inlet from Lake Huron that was almost as large as Lake Ontario—he was given final warnings. These were that he must always eat Indian food, however badly cooked or tasteless or dirty it was; that he was to be prompt in rendering small services, such as keeping a tinder box handy to light the calumets; that he must be careful not to carry sand into a canoe or splash it with water; that he was not to stand on ceremony, but help to carry baggage at a portage; that he had better not ask too many questions, and on no account criticize, but be always cheerful; that he should make a habit of giving small presents, such as beads or fishhooks. It was impressed upon him that the opinion of the Indians formed of him on the journey they would retain; moreover, that this opinion would be broadcast upon their arrival at their destination; and that it would be very hard to live it down if it were unfavorable.

The party did not take the long route of the lakes, but went up the Ottawa River to Lake Nipissing and from there down what is now called French River to the Huron settlement on Georgian Bay. As the Indians could not quite manage the name Isaac Jogues, they called him Ondessonk, "bird of prey." That it was quite inappropriate did not trouble them in the least, and the affable Jogues was rather amused. The superior of the Blackrobes already at work among the Hurons, Jean de Brébeuf, was called Echon.

With Brébeuf at the cluster of Huron encampments was another priest, and with them a few *donnés,* laymen who gave their services to the Jesuits without pay. Another class of lay assistants were the *engagés,* men who did receive a small salary as guards, hunters and handymen. Their quarters were somewhat cramped, for, though they were assigned to a birchbark cabin about fifty feet long and eighteen wide, with a door at either end (but no windows) and a vent in the roof to allow the smoke of the fire to escape, half of this was partitioned off as the chapel.

Theirs was a medium-sized cabin; at the main village of Ihonatiria there were cabins twice the size, as well as some smaller ones. These cabins were strewn about without any regularity. Though a palisades enclosed the whole village, it was kept in such poor repair that it would have offered little protection should the Iroquois prowl so far north. The reason for the negligence was that when the accumulated filth became unbearable, even by Hurons, a new village was built elsewhere. One might have supposed that they could have dumped their refuse and rubbish half a mile away, but these Indians were too lazy to clean up filth, and they did not have the slightest inkling that it caused the frequent epidemics that descended upon them.

Yet these epidemics—mostly of measles and smallpox—were the cause of the missionaries' greatest danger, as they, like the failure of crops, were often attributed to the Blackrobes' baleful magic rather than to the malignant spirits which they used to say brought evil. The utmost precaution had to be exercised in administering baptism, as that was regarded as the deadliest magic of all. That it was only administered to the dying (usually only to dying children) fully confirmed the Hurons' suspicions. "There!" they would say in effect, "those on whose head the water is poured always die."

Each cabin contained a number of families. Only the dim light and the smoke afforded slight privacy, yet everybody could not but witness all that went on. That seems to have caused the Indians no distress, for the girls were allowed to be as promiscuous as they wished before marriage, and after they were married their husbands now and then lent them to a friend. But there was no consistent viewpoint. On occasion, when a husband became jealous—with or without cause—he might cut off his wife's nose or ears.

Under circumstances which made modesty impossible, there was a good deal of quite shameless obscenity in act and speech. This was also true of many of the communal dances and of the curative dances of the medicine men. Further, the Indians were extremely superstitious about dreams: they felt themselves obliged to perform whatever they had dreamed of, however fantastic or disgusting it might be. The missionaries found this the greatest of all obstacles to their work; it was extremely hard to convince the savages that their dreams usually had no significance; that, in any event, they were not to be considered inspirations or commands from the spirits around them.

Jogues was, of course, deeply shocked by many of the things with which he now became acquainted. Dreams, however, while presenting great difficulty to the work of conversion, were too absurd to take seriously. As to other matters, Brébeuf assured him that, if there was any place where chastity was safe, it was, for any man who stood on guard, precisely among these Indians. He set it down to the protection given by the guardian angels of the Hurons. While this may well have been the case, something was surely due to the fact that these refined Frenchmen found little attraction in the women. Some of the French trappers and traders, however, were not so squeamish.

The language presented a difficulty, too. Its pronunciation seemed to come from the back of the lips, even the stomach. On the other hand, its grammar was highly elaborate, the verbs being conjugated as in Greek, but with a double conjugation, one direct, the other reciprocal; in some instances, there was also a feminine conjugation. Subtle shades of meaning were therefore possible; savages the Hurons were, but there was nothing savage about their speech.

Despite the subtlety of which their language was capable, it was almost impossible for these people to grasp abstract ideas. While they understood the difference between the red and white paint with which they bedaubed themselves, they were at a total loss if they heard about whiteness or redness. So also with strength and courage, though they were both strong and courageous. Everything, if it was to penetrate their comprehension, had to be made absolutely concrete. Even in making the sign of the cross the Hurons were permitted to change the wording to "In the name of our Father, and of His Son, and of Their Holy Spirit." Only by definite images could the most elementary truths of the faith be brought home to them. This meant that the Blackrobes had to proceed slowly; they had to be very cautious about receiving adult Indians into the Church.

Nevertheless, they did make enough converts to believe that in time the entire tribe would become Christians. Yet they knew that every day they were in danger of being murdered. Indeed, one day they were invited to a feast which they fully realized was of a ceremonial sort—one given to men who were about to be killed. But, as it was part of the ceremony that a speech was expected from the victims, Brébeuf delivered one with such superb eloquence and aplomb that, for the time being, the lives of the Frenchmen were spared. The Hurons were so impressed that they even undertook to build a church.

Rumors at last arrived that the dreaded Iroquois were planning a raid, whereupon Isaac Jogues was asked whether he would go to Quebec to inform the governor, so that his vigilance might be increased. It was made clear that this was not a command, merely a suggestion, which Jogues was perfectly free to reject. Nevertheless, he accepted the hazardous mission at once and, accompanied by the *donnés,* Guillaume Coûture and René Goupil, as well as a couple of *engagés* and a number of Indians—several of whom were Christians —he set off for Montreal. From that point they would be reasonably safe on their journey to Three Rivers and then Quebec. As there were about forty members in the party, it was hoped that the Iroquois would be deterred from making an attack.

They went by the shorter and quicker route, thinking that they would be less likely to be ambushed on it than if they followed the course of the Great Lakes. When they emerged without incident upon the broad waters of the St. Lawrence, a problem arose: should they go around the islands of Lake St. Peter by the northern channel, or take the easier, though more hazardous, southern channel? The Hurons with Jogues saw a number of footprints on the southern bank of the river, but (why, it is not at all clear) decided that they were those of friendly Algonquins. It was a fatal error of judgment, for the canoes were soon ambushed by a large party of Iroquois.

Some of the Hurons managed to escape, as did the *engagés*. Jogues could have hidden in the long grass, if he had not decided that it was his duty to give himself up, as he perhaps could baptize before their death several of those he saw to have been captured. He says in the *Relation* published in 1647: "It must be that my body suffer the fire of earth, in order to deliver these poor souls from the flames of hell; it must die a transient death, in order to procure for them eternal life." Coûture's feelings were somewhat different; he shot a chief dead with his arquebus, but was instantly overpowered, and his finger nails drawn out and his hands made pulp by Mohawk teeth. For this band was from that tribe, the fiercest of all in the confederation of the Five Nations.

The captives numbered twenty-two, the rest having been killed at the first onslaught or managing to get away. They were taken in canoes down the whole length of Lake Champlain and Lake George, then, after portages, to the Hudson, as far as the Mohawk River, the journey taking thirteen days. All understood what was in store for them, and Jogues was able surreptitiously to baptize several of the Hurons who had been taken with him, as he was also able to admit René Goupil, a former medical student, into the Society of Jesus.

The captives were tortured in several of the Mohawk villages, for these Indians did not wish to miss that delight, but they were not to suffer death until after Mohawks from other camps had taken part in the sport. For this reason the prisoners had to be kept strong enough to endure their sufferings, and, as their hands had been gnawed to pulp, they had to be fed, almost tenderly, like children. Though the tortures were varied, the action always started when the captives were stripped naked and made to run the gauntlet. Then they were placed upon a platform, where greater tortures were employed—anything that Indian ingenuity could think of. In the case of Brébeuf, when his time came, boiling water was poured over his head in mockery of baptism. In every performance lighted torches were pressed against the naked flesh, the most sensitive parts of the body being selected.

Among the Indians, both captors and captives, torture seems to have been a kind of contest, the captives enduring all with impassive stolidity, while the braves and the squaws initiated their children into the ritual of cruelty. A captive who did not flinch was greatly admired, and (in one sense) won the game. Brébeuf later was so highly regarded for the way he had endured torture that (a great posthumous compliment) the Indians (who were not cannibals) ate his heart to gain some of his courage. Jogues, after the preliminary tortures, was stretched out naked, his feet and hands tied to pegs in the ground. Then the children amused themselves by throwing bits of smoldering wood upon his body.

Coûture was "adopted" (which means enslaved) by a family in an adjoining village. Goupil, however, had his skull split by a tomahawk for having baptized an Indian infant. Jogues, who was with him at the time, knelt down to receive a similar stroke, but was told that there was no intention of killing him—not yet. He was, in fact, adopted by an Indian woman, whom he called his "aunt," and not unkindly treated.

When he searched for Goupil's body he found it in a river bed, with the flesh partly eaten by dogs, and just when he was trying to give it Christian burial it disappeared again. A long time later Jogues came across the remains, but nothing was left but the skull and some half-gnawed bones. These he kissed as the relics of a martyr and then buried, hoping that some day he might be able to take them to Three Rivers. By this time the Mohawks were talking of releasing the Blackrobe, thinking it prudent not to go too far with the French in Canada.

Though this was decided against, Jogues's life was not too harsh. However, he was aware that at any moment he might be put to death. Meanwhile, he had come to find the Indian food, for lack of anything better, "not only tolerable, but I might even say pleasant." This was with reference to "the entrails of fish . . . the intestines of the deer, full of blood and half purified excrement, fungus growths boiled in water, decayed oysters, frogs eaten whole, head and feet, not even skinned or cleaned." Though that is quite disgusting, there were other times, especially after a hunt, when there were venison and wild fowl. Unfortunately, even the most nauseous parts of deer and turkey and fish were highly regarded as condiments.

The Dutch at Fort Orange, though they were allies of the Iroquois, to the extent of finding them useful, could not but take pity upon the plight of a fellow European, even if he was a Catholic priest and they Calvinists. They contrived to get word to Jogues that, if he would come to their settlement, they would somehow get him to New Amsterdam. To go to Fort Orange was easy enough, as Jogues wes permitted to wander at large, but as soon as the Indians realized that he had fled, they naturally guessed that he had gone to the Dutch, and they angrily demanded to search every house in the settlement. Once they came within an inch of finding his hiding-place, but at last Jogues was smuggled aboard a small ship at night and reached New Amsterdam safely.

There he found another ship, and a not very sea-worthy one, for France. On Christmas Day, 1642, he reached the Jesuit college at Rennes and asked to see the rector. When the superior came into the parlor Jogues introduced himself merely as a man who had come from New France. At this the rector pricked up his ears: "Then perhaps you can tell me something about Père Jogues; we heard that he had been captured by the Indians." Upon this the visitor stretched out his mangled hands and said: "I am Jogues."

The Pope, when the news reached him, gave Jogues a special dispensation to say Mass, despite mutilated hands which ordinarily would have debarred him from the altar. The words deserve to be quoted: "It would be shameful if a martyr of Christ should not drink the blood of Christ."

Though Jogues might have stayed quietly in France resting upon his laurels he was consumed with the idea of returning to the Mohawks. And so he did. Upon his arrival at Quebec, Governor Montmagny asked him if he would go in the capacity of ambassador to the Indians. Nobody could have been more willing to do so, and now the Blackrobe was received with every display of honor by the very people who a year before had tortured him. The negotiations for peace proceeded so favorably that the ambassador felt he was able to go back to Quebec to make the announcement that all was going to be well and to obtain a formal ratification of terms.

Unluckily, he left behind a box, the key of which he carried in his pocket. The Indians, therefore, could not open it; in fact, they hardly dared to touch it, as they imagined that there was a demon inside. They picked it up very gingerly and threw it in the deepest part of the river, from which a demon, it was believed, could not escape. The reason for their change of attitude was that they had just experienced one of their frequent epidemics, for which, of course, they laid the blame upon Jogues. The ambassador, this time dressed as a priest, went back to the Mohawks, accompanied by the youthful *donné* Jean de la Lande. As they neared Ossernenon a large band of Mohawks sprang at them from the thickets, threw them to the ground, and subjected them to the beatings that were the preliminaries to torture.

Yet they were not subjected to torture, but merely held prisoners while it was debated what should be done with them. The clans of the Wolf and the Turtle argued that the peace treaty should be honored; the Bear clan thought that the captives should be killed. One of the young braves, however, decided to act on his own account, and, as he found accomplices, he invited Jogues to a feast, to which he went—against the advice of his "aunt." But as he stooped to go through the low door of the cabin, the brave's tomahawk crashed upon his skull, and he died instantly. His head was cut off, as was de la Lande's, and set upon the stockade. This happened in late October, 1646.

A little later, the murderer was captured by the French and handed over to the Algonquins, with orders that in putting him to death they were not to use torture. Before his execution, just a year after the murder, the man was baptized, taking the name of Isaac Jogues.

II: Jacques Marquette
(1637–1675)

In the case of Marquette, his enormous celebrity—too great a celebrity, according to John Gilmary Shea and Father Steck—rests entirely upon a single achievement: the expedition he made to explore the river now known as the Mississippi. That he undertook this was perhaps due to a lucky chance that came his way, though it seems to have been something he had long dreamed about. Had it not been for this journey he would have been merely one of a host of Jesuit missionaries, indistinct figures about whom we know next to nothing, except that they devoted their lives to the salvation of the Indians.

As this expedition has rightly come to mean so much, some notice should be given to what led up to it. In 1528, Panfilo de Narváez, a tall red-bearded soldier who had served under Cortés, landed at Tampa Bay. He pressed inland with a small force, and after some clashes with the Indians returned to the harbor where he had left his ships. He found that they had given him up as lost and had sailed away. There was nothing for it but to build as best they could five small boats, using whatever materials were at hand. They killed their horses, using their tails and manes for rigging, their skins as bottles to hold water, and their flesh as food—and set out, hoping to get to Mexico. As they went westward the force of the current emerging from an unknown estuary drove them out to sea; they had discovered that an incredibly great river opened into the gulf. Most of the men in this expedition were lost at sea, as may be easily imagined, but Alvar Nuñez Cabeza de Vaca and five others were captured by the Indians, rising in their esteem because of the healing powers with which they were credited. Cabeza de Vaca eventually escaped (after six years), and reached Mexico by land, after crossing the Colorado and the Rio Grande. He wrote an account of his adventures and named the river which he never saw, though he was aware that it was tremendous, the Espiritu Santo.

Cabeza de Vaca's *Relation,* however, was an incentive to Hernando de Soto, Pizarro's second-in-command during the conquest of Peru. Though he did not set out to explore, but rather to conquer for Spain all the territory to the north, then vaguely known as Florida, he did reach the river and cross it, in flat boats of his own making, at a point somewhat below the present Memphis. Further explorations followed—always in the hope of finding the kind of treasures he had seen in Peru—but de Soto died, still in his forties, and was buried secretly at night in the great river he had discovered. The survivors of his expedition, after failing to reach Mexico by way of Texas, built boats like Narváez. Half of the original force of 600 reached their objective.

As two of the survivors wrote vivid and detailed accounts of de Soto's expedition, the existence of the Mississippi was definitely known. The Spaniards, however, and later the French, thought that there might be a river still greater which emptied into the Pacific and so would give quick access to China and India. Though a contemporary map shows more rivers than there actually were—all flowing into the gulf or the Atlantic and none showing a Pacific outlet—it has been suggested that this was a deliberate attempt to throw other nations off the scent. This seems a little far-fetched; it is much more likely that the inexpert cartographer indicated what he knew, or had heard about, but also did some guessing. At all events, the full significance of the Mississippi was hidden, and it was considered to be quite possible that the "great river" of which the seventeenth-century Jesuits had heard from some of the Indians did flow into the Pacific.

There the matter rested for about a hundred years. The Spanish dream of gold mines on the northern continent had long since evaporated. The English colonies on the Atlantic seaboard do not seem to have been much interested in exploration, having all that they could handle where they were. And the French trappers had a wonderful waterway for their furs along the Great Lakes and the St. Lawrence. The missionaries, however, thought about tribes they might evangelize farther west, and the governor of New France well understood what it would mean to his king if he could find a passage to Asia.

While primarily concerned with saving souls, the missionaries were not indifferent to their country's interests; nor were the secular administrators indifferent to the conversion of the savages. Civilization and Christianization were almost interchangeable terms; about that the governor at Quebec and the Jesuits were in accord. Even if there were no waterway to the Pacific, this mysterious great river should be explored, as it might bring other rich territories under the control of France and other souls under the lordship of Christ. But until the time of Marquette there was no suitable man available for what had to be undertaken.

Now for the facts as to Marquette. He was born on June 10, 1637, in Laon in the south of France, of a noble but not rich family. As commonly happened to such youths—it had happened to Isaac Jogues thirty years earlier—he was sent to one of the Jesuit colleges which enjoyed so great a prestige. Unlike most of his fellow students, he enrolled in the Society of Jesus. He had, of course, no idea as to what work he would be eventually assigned, nor had his superiors. One might add that, while a Jesuit is perfectly free to indicate what field of labor he prefers, he is also expected to hold himself ready to do whatever he is told.

Natural endowments are realistically taken into consideration in the appointments made. We are told that young Marquette showed linguistic ability while at college, and this may have weighed with those who sent him to New France, where the Indians had many different tongues. Whatever bearing Marquette's flair for languages had in the matter, it was observed in the novitiate and the house of studies that he showed more than a usual interest in the *Jesuit Relations*. This was a series of annual volumes containing letters from the missionaries in Canada. They report not only about the work they were doing, but give intensely interesting accounts of the Indian tribes, as well as information about the climate, the suitability of the soil for this or that crop, the kind of food obtainable, and the animals, especially those whose fur was valuable. There were also maps of a rough sort—not always very accurate, but still of some use—and appeals for funds and recruits.

In some ways the *Relations* were like missionary magazines of our own time. They were, however, a good deal more than that, as they contained ethnological information of the highest importance, as well as a certain amount of history. The missionaries were all men of excellent education, and they had wonderful opportunities for studying the manner of life of the savages among whom they were working. This they set down with the utmost fidelity, for the whole point of their writing was that their superiors in France be fully posted about conditions in New France. For this reason the *Relations* constitute indispensable source material to the historian of Canada in the seventeenth century. While the secular administrators also made reports, they did not have the missionaries' close contacts with the Indians, though they sometimes told of matters about which the missionaries were unaware or in which they had relatively little interest. Moreover, official reports were usually statistical and dry; the *Relations* are consistently fascinating.

Jacques Marquette had probably long thought of this missionary field for himself and had frequently spoken of it as where he would like to be. But the same thing could be said, no doubt, of other young Jesuits, whom their superiors nevertheless decided should remain in France or go to the Orient. Marquette, however, got what he wished; on September 20, 1666, he set sail for Quebec.

He remained in that settlement just long enough to receive instructions. Then he was sent about thirty miles west to Three Rivers, an important trading station, and there he was given some lessons in the language of the Montagnais. As it was noticed that he was physically not very robust, it was thought that he was not well fitted for life in the woods, though his natural gaiety and his affability were seen to be good equipment for a missionary anywhere. He was thirty-one when he was sent to Sault de Sainte Marie, in the territory of the Ottawas, and on the channel connecting Lakes Superior and Huron, afterwards going to Michillimackinac Island, where Lakes Huron and Michigan meet.

There, or perhaps somewhere nearby on the mainland, Père Marquette built a little birch-bark chapel and began his work among the Hurons. They were friendly enough to the Blackrobes, as they looked upon the French as their protectors against the Iroquois and the Sioux, though unfortunately there were not enough soldiers in New France at that time to prevent their virtual extermination.

About Marquette's work as a missionary we have little positive information, though we may be sure that it was devoted. Perhaps it attracted little attention because it was done in relatively easy circumstances, not amid the hardships of the deep woods. In any event, it is not as a missionary that he is now remembered, but as an explorer.

On his journey to the west Marquette had seen, a little beyond Montreal, the rapids known as La Chine. The name had been given because it had been imagined that the St. Lawrence and the Great Lakes led on, with portages, to a river that gave access to the Pacific and therefore to China.

Nor was this idea entirely fallacious. The Illinois, when Marquette encountered them, were not well informed as to the course of the upper reaches of the Missouri, or as to its length, yet there was a means of reaching the Gulf of California by means of that river and the Platte and Colorado. It was not a very serviceable route, but, with portages, it did exist.

The design of exploring the great river about which Marquette had several times been told became more definite when a young officer named Louis Joliet was appointed by the governor in Quebec to head an expedition. He had often talked about the project with Marquette, who probably even inspired him to undertake it. However that may be, he was perfectly willing to take the Jesuit along. For one thing, the priest was young—only thirty-three—and friendly and fearless; for another, he knew six Indian languages, an invaluable qualification.

Joliet was a young man of excellent character. He had been educated in France by the Jesuits and at one time had thought of joining them, but instead had gone out to New France in the employment of the Company of the Hundred Associates. By them he had been used to locate copper mines and in the fur trade, during which time he became well acquainted with a country but little known and struck up his friendship with Père Marquette. Francis Parkman may be right in saying that he did not have much capacity for command, but, as this expedition was not of a military nature, the good qualities he did possess were considered quite sufficient by Comte de Frontenac, Governor of New France. The *Relation* for 1673 reported: "He has both tact and prudence, which are the chief characteristics required for the success of a voyage as dangerous as it is difficult. He has the courage to dread nothing where everything is to be feared." Though Marquette was not entrusted with the command, which was always given to a soldier, it was probably understood that he would be the real leader and the soul of the undertaking.

A priest normally went with such an exploring party. This was because the French never neglected the possibility of converting the savages; further, his presence would be useful in the maintenance of discipline. That these two men were accompanied by five *donnés* obliges us to consider the exploration of the Mississippi a Jesuit project, even though Joliet had been placed in nominal command by Frontenac.

The preparations for the voyage were carefully made. As they might reach a district where they would run out of food, they provided themselves with a quantity of corn and dried meat. They were to go in two canoes: Marquette in one and Joliet in the other. And as exploration was their object—locating where the great river reached the sea—they took along astronomical instruments and all that was needed for the making of maps and writing down a record of the journey. Every possible precaution was considered, so that, as Marquette's account was to say, "if our undertaking was hazardous, it should not be foolhardy." Joliet allowed himself ample time to talk over the plans with Marquette, and also to question the Indians as to what they knew about the rivers—all of which information was put in writing for their guidance—so it is abundantly evident that, while these explorers were brave, they were in no sense rash.

There were various theories about what we now call the Mississippi River. Marquette, in a letter he wrote to his superior at Quebec, expressed doubts as to whether the river had its mouth in the Gulf of California, though he by no means excluded that possibility, or that of an estuary in Chesapeake Bay. What he did not doubt at all was that to know definitely where it did empty would be very useful. He inclined to what turned out to be the right answer: that the river flowed, more or less in a straight line, due south and into the Gulf of Mexico.

The Indians were astonished at the hardihood of Marquette and Joliet and the five *donnés,* and warned them that they might run into all kinds of unforeseen difficulties and dangers. Yet two of them offered to act as guides as far as the Missouri, from which point they would return home. Even that much assistance was gratefully welcomed. All these young high-spirited men knew that this was going to be a great adventure.

They left Marquette's headquarters at St. Ignace on May 17, 1673. Their fears that they might run out of food turned out to be unnecessary. They even came across a friendly tribe, which had paddy fields of rice, and this was a welcome change from the tasteless and monotonous sagamité of corn, whether the rice was boiled or ground into flour and eaten as porridge. The rivers, too, had plenty of fish that were good eating, and for the first time they saw buffalo—as many as 400 in a herd—which they described in accurate detail. They were not the first white explorers to come across these animals, for they had been seen by Cabeza de Vaca and by the de Soto and Coronado expeditions, but theirs was the fullest account of the "wild cattle."

A friendly Indian tribe the explorers encountered insisted upon feasting them, though in a way that almost took away their appetites. The savage hosts would blow upon the cooked fish until it was cool, then put the food into the mouths of their guests. It would have been considered gross impoliteness to show any sign of repugnance at an attention meant to be courteous. They did, however, find some pretext of avoiding the next dish—which was dogflesh; it needed a de Smet to develop a relish for that. So they were served with buffalo, instead, the choicest—that is, the most disgustingly fat—morsels being placed in their mouths. These they gulped down somehow, as they understood that a high compliment was being shown.

It was on June 17 that they at last reached the Mississippi, after coming down several rivers and getting from one to the other by portages. So far they had run across friendly Indians, but they were now warned that those lower down the river might be of a different character. This they found to be the case. They were not directly attacked, but arrows were often shot in their direction from the shore. They had to be very careful where they landed; it always had to be in some remote place, far from an Indian camp.

Apart from the danger from Indians, Marquette and Joliet were sure that, if they went to the mouth of the river, they would meet Spaniards who would take them captive. There was no sense in putting themselves into unnecessary jeopardy, as by this time they had obtained much of the information they desired. They had established that the Mississippi discharged into the Gulf of Mexico and not into the Gulf of California or the Chesapeake. They had for a while inclined to a Virginian estuary, but that could now be ruled out with absolute certainty, for the Virginia seacoast is at 34 degrees latitude, whereas they had reached 33 degrees 40 minutes, and they knew that the Gulf of Mexico was at the latitude of 31 degrees 60 minutes, about two or three days' journey away. In other words, they were farther south than the place where de Soto and his army had crossed what they had known as the Rio del Espíritu Santo, and they had had good reason to learn how redoubtable were the local tribes. Marquette and Joliet therefore decided to return to their starting point.

Though Père Dablon, when writing to Paris, said that the river which had just been explored was "very probably" the one geographers called the Saint Esprit, there could hardly have been any doubt in the minds of the explorers themselves. Enough time was spent at St. Ignace to transcribe into a formal narrative the notes they had made, and, when this had been done, Joliet set out with his account (which included some maps, even if there was a good deal of guesswork in these) to hand everything over to Governor Frontenac.

Tragedy then struck the expedition—an occurrence which

gave Marquette chief honors—which he probably would have obtained in any event—and cost Joliet some of the glory he otherwise would have obtained. On the La Chine rapids, within sight of Montreal, a sudden squall capsized his canoe. Two of the men with him were lost and all the precious documents, and Joliet saved his own life only by clinging to a rock for four hours. However, he was able to gain consolation from the realization that Père Marquette had also written an account of the expedition. In Quebec, with Père Dablon's assistance, Joliet wrote down as much as he could remember. The same Père Dablon was to write of Marquette: "He was a Frenchman with the French, a Huron with the Hurons, an Algonquin with the Algonquins. He disclosed his mind with childlike candor to his superiors, and he was open and ingenuous in his dealings with all men." It is impossible to imagine, as some have charged, that such a man would have tried to rob Joliet of fame, though, of course, there could have been an honest mistake on the part of others as to the authorship of the full-length report. As for Marquette, he had written to Dablon: "I have no fear and no anxiety. One of two things must happen: either God will adjudge me a coward, or He will give me a share in His cross, which I have not yet carried since I came to this land. I hold myself surrendered to His will."

These words contain the very man, but after the expedition down the Mississippi there is nothing much to record, nothing that would not seem almost an anticlimax. We know that he lived for a while in a little cabin on the site of what is now Chicago, the first white man to go there. He and two *donnés* occupied that cabin during the winter of 1674-75. In the spring the three men were on their way to Michillimackinac when, near the present Ludington, Michigan, the midway point between Chicago and St. Ignace, Marquette felt too ill to go farther. Ill though he was and near death, he heard the confession of his companions, and then promised to call them, should there be occasion, by ringing the Mass bell. A few hours later he did ring the bell, and when the *donnés* hurried to him, he asked that the crucifix he wore round his neck be held before his eyes. When this was done he was heard to say: *"Sustinuit anima mea in verbo ejus,"* and then: *"Mater Dei, memento mei."* As Marquette was silent after that, the watchers thought that he had breathed his last, and one of them cried: "Jesus! Mary!" At this the dying man opened his eyes and, repeating the same words, "Jesus, Mary," gave his spirit into the hands of God.

III: Kateri Tekakwitha

(1656–1680)

Kateri Tekakwitha was born some time in 1656 in the Indian village of Ossernenon on the south bank of the Mohawk River about thirty miles west of Albany. She remained in this locality until in her teens she managed to make her way to a Christian Indian settlement on the south bank of the St. Lawrence, slightly west of Montreal. There she died and there her remains are carefully preserved in the hope of her eventual canonization.

The Mohawks, the tribe of the Five Nations to which Tekakwitha belonged, were agrarian, in the sense that they depended more on agriculture than on hunting for their food. They built their towns in an irregular triangle, behind a strong double palisade. As Gandawagué, where Kateri lived, had a palisade not much more than 250 feet long, the houses it contained—and the people there—must have been closely packed together. The houses, built of birch bark with a curved roof, were each occupied by four or five families, with a door at either end, and a vent in the roof for the smoke.

Because of the absence of privacy there was a great deal of shameless obscenity. Some of this Kateri must often have witnessed; nor could she close her eyes to the talk. However, as she had been left extremely short-sighted, following a bad case of smallpox while she was hardly more than an infant, this preserved her delicate modesty from being as wounded as it would have been had she possessed normal vision. Her defective eyesight also prevented her from playing with the other children of the village. All this induced in her a feeling of insecurity, and therefore prepared her to turn quite naturally to the comfort of God, even while she was still a pagan.

The ravages of smallpox also left her not at all good looking, a disadvantage which became, from her point of view, an advantage, as few young braves would want such a wife. Nevertheless, some did, because she was so gentle and eager to be of assistance to others; it was with difficulty that she deferred marriage. Early in life she determined to preserve a life-long virginity. While the Jesuits she subsequently met commended this, they could not approve her positive abhorrence for marriage, though here it is possible that they read into what she said more than she really meant. The reason for Kateri's repugnance they probably guessed. The hideous sights and indecent talk all around her, which other Indian girls took for granted, deeply shocked Kateri.

Because of her semi-blindness she was exempted from agricultural work. This was relegated to women not, as some have supposed, because they were despised by their men folk, but because women were considered as embodying the principle of fertility. A man was useful for bringing in game (and now and then a scalp), but the tribal structure was matriarchal. It was for this reason that marriage was so often pressed on Kateri.

An additional reason was that a husband became a member of his wife's family and took up his abode with them the moment that the very simple marriage ceremony had taken place; then he became a provider of meat. As Kateri had been brought up by an uncle and aunt—her father and mother having died while she was still an infant—these adopted parents were even more anxious than natural parents would have been that this source of supply be obtained. It was beyond their comprehension why the girl should object to being married; but, though they had all the authority of parents, they found their adopted daughter immovable.

She was shy and as removed from the life teeming around her as it was possible to be; as time went on, her shyness grew more marked, so that she came to be looked upon as a complete oddity, and knew herself to be different; which resulted in a further withdrawal into herself. Yet she was always helpful, invariably doing what she was asked to do, if merely a hint came, and often anticipating the small tasks within her power to perform. Actually, there was not much that was within her capacity; the mending of moccasins and wampum belts was something she was very good at, but the supply needed was limited; as for the stirring of a pot, that even a very little girl could do.

The marriage against which she had set her face, began with the simplest arrangements. Usually, the parents of the couple arranged everything; all the girl had to do was to accept a bowl of food from a suitor, and she was married, without further ceremony. Whenever Kateri was offered this symbolic food, she rushed out of the house in what people considered ridiculous alarm. Once a stern method was adopted to bring her to her senses: a young brave threatened to kill her unless she accepted him. This was probably bluff, and quite possibly Kateri's uncle and aunt were parties to the scheme. But, frightened though the girl was, quite expecting the tomahawk to cleave her skull, she would not change her attitude.

Her mother had been an Algonquin captive, spared because one of the braves needed a wife. She had been baptized, though her knowledge of the Christian faith doubtless was very sketchy. It did not extend to her knowing that she —or anybody—was quite capable of administering baptism. She died leaving her baby daughter unchristened. Kateri Tekakwitha reached young womanhood a pagan, in a village completely pagan.

It was worse than that; it was fiercely savage. Every now and then a group of captives were brought in and tortured on a raised platform (so that everybody could have a good view of the proceedings) before being burned at the stake. Kateri was well aware what was going on, for she could not avoid hearing the shouts and songs and jeers of the torturers, and sometimes a wild scream from one of the victims. Even small children were encouraged to take part in what was a ritual performance. On these occasions Kateri would creep into the darkest corner of the cabin and hold her hands over her ears. This was considered further oddity on her part.

In October 1666, when she was about ten, the French, who had recently received reinforcements in Canada, came down with a force of 600 men. The Mohawks submitted at once, without a fight. One of the conditions of the peace imposed by the French commander was that a priest be received by the tribe. But Kateri hid herself even from him. She was naturally Christian, but did not ask for the baptism that was, after some instruction, administered to others. It would seem that when she finally escaped to Canada it was, in large part, to evade the increasing insistence that she marry, though she must also have picked up bits of information from the newly baptized among the Indian women. Fragmentary though this information must have been, and Kateri's grasp of it imperfect, she realized that Christianity answered the secret needs of her heart. Her natural spiritual insight may be presumed to have perceived implications that escaped people better instructed than she was at that time.

She had also suffered from the pressures of another device that was used to force her into marriage—calumny. She had several times been threatened, sometimes by groups of drunken braves. She took refuge from such in the chapel, though she knew her persecution would be renewed. The hardest thing to bear was that her aunt sought out the priest and told him that Kateri was committing adultery with her uncle. It had been hoped that, in order to clear her name, she would marry one of the braves who had asked for her. The "proof" the woman offered was that Kateri once (and inadvertently) did not refer to her uncle as "father," but used his own name. But the priest at once saw through the plot, for he knew to what Kateri was being subjected, and sharply reprimanded the scandal-monger.

The situation became so unbearable in the Mohawk village that Kateri became desperate. It is a wonder how the shy timid girl had endured it so long. So, after her baptism —which was on Easter Sunday, April 18, 1676—she sought refuge in flight. The priest had probably made the necessary arrangements, and certainly a Christian Huron had come to be her escort to Canada, where she found a safe refuge in the Christian Indian village of Caughnawaga near Montreal. There she hoped to be free of molestation.

Yet, even there, she did not escape pressure to marry, or even instances of calumny, although her situation considerably eased. It was now thought that at Caughnawaga, as all its inhabitants were Christians, she would find an acceptable husband. As all Indian girls did marry, it was supposed that now she would drop her former objections to the married state. But Kateri's aversion remained, in spite of the advice of her new friends.

The ideal of virginity was for Kateri the key to her whole life, and was the basis of the spirituality she attained. From the outset the priests at Caughnawaga recognized that Kateri was a girl who, while only recently a pagan, was already far advanced in divine things, rudimentary as may have been her knowledge of many of the elements of faith. This appears in the fact that for her the time of probation demanded between baptism and first Communion was greatly shortened at the advice of Père Cholonec, her spiritual director. This might have resulted in a good deal of criticism had not everybody in the Christian village perceived that Kateri was so unusual a person that it was only right that she should receive special privileges.

However, it did not prevent a new calumny from occurring, though this time it sprang not from malice but from suspicion and jealousy. It was set in circulation by a new arrival at the village named Nemahbin, who as yet knew little of Kateri. She and her husband shared a cabin with Kateri. The man, coming into the long dark house late at night and very tired, threw himself down at once to sleep. In the morning Nemahbin found him lying too close to Kateri—so she considered—and put the worst construction on matters, this though the man had been an exemplary Christian for twenty years. The explanation apparently did not occur to her that in the darkness he could not see where he was lying, or even that in sleep he might have accidentally rolled a little in her direction. Had this been all, the baleful seed might never have taken root, but Nemahbin fancied that several other subsequent incidents—all quite harmless—confirmed her suspicions.

Even so, the woman did not immediately divulge what she was thinking, but waited for the return of the Blackrobe. The priest, seeing that she was genuinely troubled, listened to all that she had to say, but took the first opportunity of questioning Kateri. Her guileless face alone made him feel that there must have been some mistake; yet, as the accusation was serious, and evidently made in good faith, he told her exactly what was being said, and asked her if it was true. The frank and open way in which she made a complete denial, without showing any indignation about the ugly story, convinced him that it was totally without foundation.

So far was it from doing Kateri any permanent harm that on the following Easter, which was the anniversary of her baptism, Père Cholonec surprised her—and gave everybody in the village a signal proof of his belief in her innocence—by admitting her, on his own initiative, into the Confraternity of the Holy Family, a select group that Indians ordinarily could join only after years of blameless life. Kateri, in her humility, was overwhelmed and declared herself unworthy of the distinction. But, as the Blackrobe persisted, the girl, who had been deeply wounded in the calumny brought against her, consented. She realized that it would finally crush all suspicions.

Life at Caughnawaga was quiet and uneventful. Yet it was Indian life in everything except that this was a wholly Catholic community. The homes were long, low, curved-roofed birchbark cabins. While there was a certain amount of hunting and fishing, the Blackrobes did all they could to promote the cultivation of a few easily raised crops, mostly corn and peas and beans. The settlement was far enough away from Montreal to prevent many white visitors from going there. The Blackrobes did not encourage contacts between the Indians and the French, knowing only too well how easily their neophytes could fall under the power of fire-water.

Sometimes, however, a small group from Caughnawaga would visit Montreal. Kateri and a few other young women dropped in at the school conducted by Blessed Marguerite Bourgeois, now a flourishing college for girls. At that time its curriculum was elementary, but a number of Indian girls attended on a footing of equality with the whites. It specially interested the visitors, who spent several days at the Villa Maria Convent, that several Indians were already seeking admission into the community. They were being held back only because it was considered advisable that they should first have further training. For the support of the Indian students an annual donation was made by the King of France, the wise French policy being that of assimilating them as soon as possible. It was evident that they were apt pupils, and their piety was equally evident.

Not surprisingly, Kateri and one of her friends, a girl

named Marie Thérèse, were inspired with the idea of building a birch-bark cabin on Heron Island, a dot of land in the middle of the river. There they could find retirement and perhaps eventually be able to build up an Indian sisterhood. But the priests, when they were consulted, smiled gently at so ill-considered, if natural, an idea. While it was true that the group might be able to raise a few crops, possibly all that they needed for their food, it was unlikely that they would find the seclusion they were picturing, as both Indians and whites would come over in droves to gaze with curiosity at this wonder. Besides, they were still too young in the faith for a venture of this sort. Disappointed, but recognizing that the Blackrobes were only talking good sense, Kateri and her friend abandoned the scheme.

The idea, even if it had been approved, was extremely dangerous. When the Iroquois began a new war against the French, they tried to get those in the Christian settlement to join them. When this alliance was refused, the pagan Indians turned in their fury against the Christians of their own blood, carrying off several captives. These they subjected to torture before burning them at the stake. It was obviously unsafe for a few young women to be anywhere except in the village, where they would have some protection.

Later, some of those at Caughnawaga adopted some extreme forms of asceticism, of a physical and quite unauthorized sort, the women going farther than the men. We hear of them wandering along the bank of the St. Lawrence in mid-winter dressed only in their shifts and of saying the rosary in sub-zero temperatures. Not satisfied with that, others chopped holes in the frozen river and stayed there up to their necks in the icy water saying their prayers; one woman even immersed her baby in this fashion, so that it almost died. The pagan Indians went in for somewhat similar austerities, so as to inure their bodies; the motive of these Christians was, of course, quite different, yet the form of their penances bore too close a resemblance to pass unreproved. Besides, these mortifications were often highly injudicious. It had never been part of the Jesuit idea to give approval to self-imposed physical sufferings, but rather to accept, as from God's hand, whatever pain came, and to impose upon one's self only interior mortifications.

Kateri Tekakwitha herself did not avoid such things—which, indeed, other Indians expected of her—but she usually went no farther than to sleep upon thorns or to sprinkle ashes upon a sagamité that was already, one would have supposed, sufficiently lacking in flavor. Père Cholonec, when he heard of what was going on, though he admired Kateri's motives, gave her a good scolding for her imprudence, and ordered her to throw the thorns under her mat into the fire. The saying of prayers up to one's neck in icy water—especially such an embroidery upon that penance as putting an infant into that water—he peremptorily forbade.

For Kateri, Père Cholonec decided that there was a penetential road at once safer and more meritorious. He had long been aware that she wished to live and die a virgin, and he recommended that she might add to her merit by doing this bound by a vow. She took a vow of virginity—privately, of course—on the Feast of the Annunciation, March 25, 1679. After that, the question of her marrying was closed in the eyes of the whole community.

Her aversion to the thought of marriage, even while she was a pagan, was due to the shocks her delicate and refined nature had received, but was merely of a natural kind. Since she had come to live at Caughnawaga as a Christian, her love of virginity belonged in the supernatural order. She still was advised to marry, even by the couple with whom she lived. They attempted nothing like the former bullying and trickery, but her foster sister in the kindest and most reasonable way told her that, while she was most welcome to stay with them, she should insure herself against the precariousness of life. They had a large family, but, if anything should happen to the father of the family, what would become of her? Marriage was the normal mode of life, and matrimony was a sacrament: why, then, this strange repugnance?

After several such discussions by her foster sister, Kateri took the question to Père Cholonec. While he perfectly understood that the intentions of Kateri's foster sister were excellent, and that there was much to be said in favor of her arguments, he was not so sure that they bore on Kateri's very special case. Even so, he would not presume to pronounce definitely, but told Kateri that this was a question that she had to decide for herself. All he suggested was that she give the matter further careful thought; when he saw that her mind was quite made up, he consented to her taking a vow of virginity.

Except that we know that she spent much of every day praying in the woods, we have little knowledge of her interior life. Kateri was not very articulate, and whatever she confided to Père Cholonec he, as her confessor, was not free to divulge. In the life he wrote of her he was obliged to use only such generalities as everybody knew. But one small point speaks volumes; though everybody in the village was a Christian, everybody spoke of Kateri as *the* Christian. The other Indians liked to kneel near her in the chapel, because they felt that this made them pray more fervently. She seemed to bear a special sort of effulgence.

The following year Kateri died. That year we may be sure was the happiest of her life, for not only did she become closer to God than ever, but her vow had released her from the importunities that had so often distressed her. Cholonec observed that her natural gaiety, which had so often been smothered under her worries, was now allowed free vent. It was not that she suddenly turned from a rather unhappy to a merry maiden, but she wore a look of serenity and content.

Even the fact that life at Caughnawaga was quiet and uneventful exactly suited her disposition.

In spite of a somewhat sickly childhood she had grown up to be rather notably vigorous. Yet during the winter hunt early in 1680 she fell sick, and, as the other members of the Confraternity of the Holy Family had accompanied the hunting party, there was nobody to nurse her. The only people left in the village were a few elderly and infirm women, and it was about as much as they could do to look after their own wants. A bowl of gruel and a cup of water were brought to her from time to time, but that was about all. As the Blackrobe was himself absent for much of that time, there was nobody to prepare her for the death she knew to be approaching.

When the Jesuit did return, he saw at a glance that he would have to hasten. The custom there was that the dying were carried in a litter to the chapel to receive Viaticum. Partly because there were not enough able-bodied persons in Caughnawaga to carry her (though this could have been managed), but more because Kateri's was an exceptional case, Père Cholonec brought Viaticum to her in her own cabin. This was on April 16, 1680. By this time some of the members of the hunting party had returned, for we hear of Kateri's friend Marie Thérèse lending her a tunic for the great occasion, a tunic better than any that Kateri possessed. She felt that she should receive her Lord in the finest clothes obtainable. A few days later she was dead.

Where they buried her beside the St. Lawrence became, though, of course, quite unofficially, a kind of shrine. As the Indians were convinced that she was a saint, they used to go there to pray for her intercession. Some of the French who knew about her did the same. Indeed, the first written testimonial about one of Kateri's miracles came from Captain Du Luth, commandant at Fort Frontenac, after whom the city of Duluth, Minnesota, has been named. On August 15,

1696, he made a statement that most explicitly declares that Kateri cured him of his long-standing gout at the end of a novena he had made in her honor and had promised to visit her grave if his health was restored.

Perhaps it was in order to avoid even the appearance of a public cultus, as this might prove detrimental to her cause for beatification, that her bones have been removed from her grave and are now kept in the sacristy of the Jesuit church in Caughnawaga.

IV: Junípero Serra

(1713–1784)

Californians recognize that the Franciscan missionary, Junípero Serra, was the true founder of their State. Many of them are also aware that it was he, more than anybody else, who prevented the Russians from annexing part, if not all, of the Pacific coast.

Junípero Serra was born on Mallorca, the largest of the Balearic Islands, on November 24, 1713. His father, a peasant farmer, was, like his wife and children, notably devout. And young Serra from his boyhood was under the influence of the Franciscans, whose novitiate at Palma he entered. They conducted the Lullian University and there Serra obtained his degree, afterwards being appointed a professor, holding a chair in Scotist philosophy and proving himself an acceptable preacher.

His heart, however, was indifferent to academic distinction; instead, he was fired with the thought of becoming a missionary in the New World. He accordingly sailed to Mexico with his friend (afterwards his biographer), Francisco Palóu. From Mexico City, where he acted as novice master, he was sent to the mountainous region of Sierra Gorda, where he worked strenuously among the Pame Indians, making converts and supervising a cluster of churches, some of which he built himself. There he increased his reputation as an able and holy man.

It was not until Serra had been in Mexico for nearly twenty years that his chance to enter California came. This was in 1767, when King Charles III of Spain, under the influence of several infamous advisers, sent secret instructions to his dominions that they were to expel all Jesuits. He seems to have been persuaded that there was a Jesuit plot to assassinate him. Further, he had, like many people, convinced himself that the Jesuits owned vast hoards of hidden treasure. In some places they were imagined to be forcing the hapless natives to work gold or silver mines; in Lower California, the treasures were supposed to be pearls. Though pearls actually were to be found in those waters, they were so small as to be worthless.

To investigate conditions in Mexico, José de Galvez—a good Catholic, though with a strong prejudice against Jesuits—was sent out as inspector general. He was an able, energetic and honest man, who became a firm friend of the group of Franciscans who, under Serra, were selected to replace the Jesuits. Though he had too much to attend to elsewhere to be free to go to Upper California himself, he sent a company of soldiers under Captain Gaspar de Portolá to open a new mission field in what is now the State of California.

Portolá and Galvez first investigated the matter of the pearls, but found none of any value, while Serra reorganized the missions in the peninsula that formerly had been staffed by Jesuits. The Indians there were quite backward and the country itself was parched and infertile. But it was believed (as it turned out, correctly) that the land farther north was vastly superior. Back in 1603 a Spanish ship had put into Monterey and its captain, Sebastián Vizcaíno, wrote so glowing an account of its harbor that it was decided that this should become a base for further exploration. If Viscaíno entirely missed the incomparably better harbor of the present San Francisco, Francis Drake previously had also done so, no doubt in each instance because the narrow entrance was veiled by frequent fogs. Drake had landed a few miles farther north to take possession of New Albion for Queen Elizabeth I, a claim which was allowed to lapse.

Serra, leaving Palóu in charge of the former Jesuit missions, decided to go north with the main body of soldiers, all of whom were well mounted, though he himself made the arduous march on foot. This was very much of a self-denying ordinance, because, shortly after his arrival in Mexico, Serra had been bitten in the foot by a snake, but had considered the mishap so lightly that he refused medical attention. The result was that for the rest of his life he limped, all through the long journeys on foot which were so many that they became legendary.

The Spanish crown in theory supported the missionaries in the Spanish dominions, which was merely what it should have done, as the missionaries were conducting a peaceful (not to mention inexpensive) conquest. After the subjugation of the Aztecs by Cortes, the few soldiers who remained constituted hardly more than a police force. But by this time very little money for missionary work in Mexico was supplied by the king; it came instead from the interest derived from what was called the Pious Fund, an endowment to which a number of wealthy individuals had lavishly contributed. As it was administered by a commission appointed by the crown, the kings of Spain probably brought themselves to believe that their generosity was the source of the missionaries' revenue, which at one time was the case.

Serra and the friars with him needed little—hardly anything for themselves—and were never in serious difficulties because of the shortage of funds; their main difficulty was the length of time it took for supplies to reach them—that and the high-handed interference of some of the local military officers. These were already thinking of the friars as mere agents to prepare the way for the establishment of ordinary parishes, which were quite unsuitable for the Indians of California; in short, the idea of the subsequent secularization of the missions was already in the air.

Those who went up the peninsula with Serra reached San

Diego in 1769. From that point Portolá, accompanied by an engineer and surveyor named Costansó, went in search of the wonderful Monterey, which was to be their headquarters. They came across the harbor, but it little resembled the place Viscaíno had described. They were sure that they had located the right spot, but as a harbor it was so poor that it was supposed that in the intervening seventy years it had been largely filled in by drifting sand.

One of the two ships that had sailed from the peninsula had arrived at San Diego; the other had to be presumed to have been lost at sea. This and his disappointment over Monterey made Portolá almost abandon the enterprise as fruitless. Serra announced that, whatever Portolá did, he would remain at San Diego—though it is hard to see how the friars could have maintained themselves there for long. But he persuaded Portolá, along with his soldiers, to make a novena to St. Joseph that the missing ship would arrive. Sure enough, on the afternoon of March 19, the Feast of St. Joseph, a sail was seen on the horizon. Though it afterwards was lost to view, five days later the ship, the *San Antonio,* came into the roadstead of San Diego, and the California project was saved.

What had happened was that the ship, ignoring San Diego, made directly for Monterey, confident that that was where they would find Portolá and his soldiers and Serra and his friars. The ship turned back only because, when putting in for water at the Santa Barbara channel, it had lost an anchor. Had it gone on to Monterey, nobody would have been found. And had Portolá's original intention been carried out, there would have been no military force there, either, and the unprotected missionaries might have been found murdered by the California Indians. Only Serra's confidence in God had changed the situation.

The Indians of San Diego were the most intractable of all those in California, but they were mainly troublesome because of their thievish disposition, not because they were much more warlike than the Indians farther north. The truth is that these tribes—if they deserve to be given that name, for they were not organized—did not much resemble those of the English colonies and Canada, or those of the as-yet-unknown Great Plains. They had no weapons except a crude bow and a kind of boomerang. These they found useful enough for bringing down birds and rabbits, but war apparently never crossed their minds.

On July 9, 1770, Portolá and Costansó the engineer, their mission being accomplished, sailed for Mexico, the second-in-command taking charge of the soldiers and establishing his presidio—both a barracks and the seat of the secular administration—at Monterey. Serra, however, preferred to set up his own headquarters a few miles away, on the Carmel River, the name given it by the Carmelite friars who had accompanied Viscaíno. Though he did not wish the neophytes whom he had begun to gather to come into much contact with the soldiers, he accepted a small guard, under the command of a corporal, as he did at all the missions he founded.

In one of Kipling's early ballads he tells us that "single men in barracks don't grow into plaster saints," and that was to some extent true of the Spanish soldiers at the presidio. Yet one is astonished how well behaved they were upon the whole. Whether it was because of the example of the missionaries, or the strict military regulations, or the innate virtue of the men themselves, extremely few incidents of the sort that might have been expected ever occurred. What Serra found much harder was the officiousness of some of the commandants at Monterey. The title of governor had not yet been conferred, except upon the administrator in the peninsula, who theoretically had jurisdiction over Monterey, but was too far away to exercise it, and too indolent a man to wish to do so.

The man in command at Monterey was a humorless martinet named Pedro Fages, and between him and the friars things got to such a pass that Serra, who had reason to suspect that Fages opened all letters and sent on only those he wished to dispatch, decided that he had better go in person to Mexico to present his grievances to Antonio Bucarelli, the new viceroy there. This was all the more necessary because he had heard reports (which happened to be true) that Julián de Arriaga, minister of state, had indicated the possibility of supplying Upper California overland from the peninsula, and of giving up the use of ships; he had even suggested abandoning the area entirely. In any event, Serra meant to ask the viceroy to curb Fages.

In 1773 he took the next ship for San Blas, on the mainland shore of the gulf, and from there he made his way on foot to Mexico City, a long and difficult journey. Viceroy Bucarelli and his council received him most sympathetically, and at their request no less than five statements were presented in writing. He did not confine himself to the question of the relations between the missionaries and Commandant Fages, but even drew attention to the fact—mentioning names—that, as some of the soldiers in California had been there a long time, they should be recalled so that they might have the opportunity of seeing their wives and children again. He pointed out that supplies sent on from San Blas were frequently packed so carelessly that when the food reached California it was hardly edible. Furthermore, he suggested that a few carpenters and workers in metal be sent, as these would be invaluable in building churches and other structures.

As Serra was now at hand, he was questioned as to the feasibility of a shorter land route to California across the Colorado and Gila Rivers. It was Serra's opinion that this project, which had several times been suggested by Juan Bautista de Anza, a brilliant soldier and explorer, should be approved. Not long afterwards, it was carried out by a well-equipped force that took women and children with them. This was the real beginning of the Spanish colonization of California, as distinct from its military occupation and the work of the missionaries. Serra warned that the establishment of a new and better land route should not result in lessening the strength of the fleet patrolling the coast. Perhaps there was no immediate danger from Russia to the area where Serra had established himself, but the strong possibility of eventual danger was stressed. Alaska itself did not much matter, as it was a couple of thousand miles to the north. Even so, Russian expeditions should be carefully watched. It was an argument that weighed heavily with the viceroy and his council. Though Serra was not thinking primarily of Spain's material interests, he was not indifferent to them. And he skillfully dangled these interests before Bucarelli, even though Serra's main concern was the welfare of the missions.

Fages, who was a protégé of Galvez, was withdrawn and sent elsewhere, but as he was known to be an able and conscientious officer, he was given an office which he could look upon as a promotion. The viceroy and his council did not accept Serra's recommendation as to a successor, but appointed Captain Rivera. The new appointment did not prove very happy, for, though Rivera was sent instructions to help and not hamper the friars, he was of so dilatory a disposition (with stubbornness beneath it) that in many ways he was worse than Fages.

It is not necessary to enumerate by name all the missions that Serra eventually founded, which stretched all the way from San Diego to San Francisco. It is enough to say that from his headquarters at San Carlos Borromeo in Carmel the work of establishing these missions, and of supervising their work, meant that Serra had to be increasingly on the move, always going on foot along the Camino Real, a distance of 700 miles.

In every one of the missions it was insisted upon by the missionaries that the land occupied, together with all buildings and implements and any cattle or fowls, belonged to the neophytes gathered there, and that the padres were only the trustees. But it was not easy to get the idea of ownership—especially of collective ownership—into the heads of these primitive people. They could grasp "This is my hut" or "These are my bows and arrows," but the concept of the ownership of land was beyond them; they had to be educated up to it.

No Indian was ever compelled to enter a mission, though it was understod that, once he had done so, he was not free to leave; and if any of the neophytes ran away, soldiers were sent after them. No serious difficulties arose, as the young man or girl who had decamped was glad, after a few days of Indian squalor, to return to the comforts of the mission. In fact, as likely as not, he would be accompanied by some of his friends, who wished to enjoy the same comforts. In short, these neophytes were regarded as apprentices, who served a term (though an indefinite one) by way of preparation for a more mature mode of life.

Clustered around the mission stockade—built not to keep the neophytes in but to mark the boundary of the compound, and for defensive purposes, should the occasion ever arise—were the huts of the young couples who until marriage had been under the mission discipline. Though the girls (and even the married women, when their husbands happened to be away) slept in what was called the "nunnery," this was only for their protection. The neophytes married very young, choosing their partners freely. The friars often suggested partners, and these were almost always acceptable, as the Indians did not have the romantic ideas prevalent in our society.

Among the pagan Indians there was no marriage ceremony whatever; any couple who went to live together were *ipso facto* married. Polygamy was not general, but some men had several wives; commonly, they were sisters, and not infrequently the mother also joined the harem, as that was the most convenient arrangement for all concerned. A man did not have to be rich for this; all he had to do was to bring in an extra rabbit and basket of berries or acorns; his wives did such primitive cooking as was done.

The Indian men usually went naked; if the weather was cold, they coated themselves with mud. The women, who were more modest, wore a small apron in front and another behind, with a small cape over the shoulders. Those under the direction of the friars in the missions wore skirts and blouses, and these the padres themselves had to make until the Indian girls acquired some skill with the needle. Serra was rather fond of this tailor work, and gave to it any spare moment he had.

The Indian huts consisted of rushes strewn on poles, with a shallow, saucer-like excavation inside. All were verminous; when they became too verminous, the Indians burned them down and built others—in no more than an hour or two. The padres allowed the married couples to follow the Indian mode if they preferred it. While some, after having lived in the more substantial and vastly cleaner houses of the mission, built somewhat better huts and made a little effort to keep them clean, this commonly did not last long, as it was too much trouble.

Slatternly though most Indian women were, they had gentle and affectionate dispositions. And even among the completely untutored savages most married couples were faithful to their partners, not because they felt moral restraint, but because they were listless. When Spanish soldiers left the service and settled down on farms of their own, they were encouraged to marry Indian girls—there were no others available—and these unions almost invariably turned out well. It was the same with the groups of colonists in the pueblos; when one of them became a widower because of the death of his Spanish wife, he soon discovered that an Indian girl, whatever shortcomings she might have, was so gentle and so anxious to please as fully to make up for what she otherwise lacked. The Spaniards who did marry Indian girls always took one who, having learned a great deal in the missions, was hardly to be considered a savage. Such girls were always Christians.

Mortality among the young was high, chiefly because the

Indians lived with their families in such small and fetid huts. But it was also high in the missions, as it was hard to check any epidemic that started there. The friars obtained a few simple remedies and, like all missionaries among primitive people, found that they had to acquire some elementary medical knowledge.

One of the problems was to get the Indians to work. They were by nature lazy and in their savage state they spent in idle gossip most of the time they were not sleeping. For their few simple wants they could without much effort obtain all the small game and fish they needed; the lazier among them contented themselves mostly with roots or berries or the acorns their women pounded into a kind of paste. Even their few games were of a most unstrenuous sort. Only in their dances did they bestir themselves; they were ready to dance far into the night to the tune of what they considered musical instruments. At the missions these dances were curtailed, otherwise the padres would have got little sleep.

Yet, the missionaries did manage to get their neophytes to do some work, both for the needs of the mission and because work was a useful discipline. But the neophytes were certainly not overworked, from four to six hours a day being all that were needed. The missionaries rightly thought that the amount of work performed was of much less importance than its regularity. Yet even that was done only if a Franciscan worked in the fields with their neophytes; otherwise, before long they would lie down and go to sleep.

The burden of labor was further lessened by the fact that not only the ordinary feasts of the Church were observed but also all those of the Franciscan saints. Then, too, the neophytes were permitted holidays—not as a group, but individually. They were permitted to go home from time to time, and if some of the young men said they would like to go out for the day to hunt or fish, that was readily allowed.

The early churches were temporary wooden structures, put up rapidly by the padres, with the help of the military guard and with the neophytes carrying the timber. Before long, adobe—blocks of clay dried in the sun—was used, and the Indians became adept in handling this material, so much so that kiln-baked bricks were afterwards substituted. The design of these mission churches has often been praised. The lines were simple because the Indian builders, even under the direction of the padres, were not capable of anything elaborate. But we know from the churches that Serra had previously built in the Sierra Gorda—where skilled workmen could be obtained from Mexico City, and also because the Pame Indians were of a higher calibre than those of California—that his personal taste leaned toward the baroque. Only because he was obliged to use such materials and such workmen as were available was simplicity attained.

Eventually, some of the mission Indians became fairly good carpenters and blacksmiths, and even made tiles and pottery. They also mastered the not too difficult task of manufacturing soap and candles, and they became expert in the tanning of leather. Some of the saddles they made deserved all the admiration they have received.

A few of the neophytes learned to read and write, but as there were only two Franciscans stationed at any mission—and of these one had to work in the fields—there was little time to spare for the classroom. But all the neophytes talked Spanish—as part of the civilizing process and also for the convenience of the missionaries; there were so many dialects that people in adjoining valleys could not understand one another. To keep the neophytes amused, little dramatic performances were staged, the Indians showing that they had a flair for such things. And we know from the musical scores that have survived (with the notes in different colors to indicate the parts to be taken) that the Indians, after some training, learned to sing quite creditably.

The food supplied in the missions was, according to our ideas, monotonous and tasteless, but it was what the Indians liked. In any event it was vastly superior to the flesh of such dead whales as were washed to shore, for these the Indians would greedily devour even when it was rotting, and besmear themselves with blubber. The *atole* of barley grain made into a mush and the *pinole,* which was basically much the same except that it was mixed with nuts and berries, were nutritious. For guests arriving at the mission some meat or chicken might be served; later accounts mention that peaches and apricots and pomegranates were introduced from Mexico, probably not in sufficient quantities to be served very often. Crops of beans and chick peas were also cultivated, and the neophytes were free to have little gardens of their own. During hot afternoons the workers were refreshed with a drink made of vinegar and sweetened water. On no account were they allowed to touch intoxicants; the padres kept their little stores of wine carefully locked up.

Eventually, the missions had immense herds of cattle, as well as of horses and other livestock, and considerable prosperity was achieved even before Serra died, though it was only afterwards that their prosperity was such as to lead to their secularization by the Mexican government, ostensibly in the interests of "progress," but actually to provide venal politicians with sources of plunder. Even during Serra's latter years, he encountered troubles that pointed to still greater troubles ahead.

The arrogance and incompetence of Rivera, who had replaced Fages, caused serious difficulties. Usually lethargic, he was high-handed in his treatment of some of the rebels in a rising at San Diego. The Indians were beaten off, but one of the ringleaders took sanctuary in the chapel. Rivera, however, dragged him out, despite all protests, arguing that the place of refuge was not a sanctuary at all, but merely a storehouse, even though it was used for Mass. He was promptly excommunicated, and when he was later assassinated, he was replaced by Felipe de Neve, the first commandant to be given the title of governor.

Administrative changes in the government of Mexico enabled him to rule with a high hand. Some of the "reforms" he introduced clearly pointed to the secularization of the missions. He insisted that they be transformed into *pueblos,* with Indians elected as *alcaldes.* To make matters worse, the newly appointed Bishop Reyes of Sonora, under whose jurisdiction the Franciscan missions had passed, was in favor of the establishment of parishes, which meant a complete change in the character of the work. The bishop was quite out of touch with conditions in California, for he never so much as visited it. He did not grasp the fact that, though Serra from the beginning had thought of the missions as a training ground from which the neophytes would in time emerge into maturity, the time needed for this was a great deal longer than was envisioned, so that the new scheme was premature and unsuitable.

Furthermore, Serra had been given faculties of administering confirmation for a ten-year period. Governor Neve demanded to see the written authorization. He took this action only after Serra had already confirmed 2,000 Indians. Though, after long-drawn-out correspondence, Neve had it proved to him that the faculties actually existed, for a considerable time, completely exceeding his authority, he peremptorily forbade Serra to administer the sacrament. Serra continued more or less secretly to confirm small groups, and Neve probably was aware of this, though he found it advisable to pretend to know nothing of what was going on.

Eventually, Neve was transferred, upon which a much-subdued Fages returned, now with the title of governor. This time he and Serra got along well together. He knew that, when Serra had gone to Mexico to complain about him to the viceroy, while he was removed, he was also promoted, and he bore no grudge. During his governorship Serra confirmed an additional 3,000 persons.

Serra had by now worn himself out by incessant work.

When he got back to Carmel after he had attended the opening of the Santa Clara mission (which was for Spanish colonists, not Indian neophytes) it was noticed how weak he was. Perhaps it was because Palóu, who had been in the peninsula, but was now appointed to Santa Clara, was sure that Serra had not long to live that he went with him to his headquarters, wishing to attend his deathbed. No doubt he already intended to write Serra's life, and it was fortunate for the rounding out of the book that he was able to give an eye-witness account of his friend's last days.

One of the surprising things Palóu relates was that on the morning of his death, Serra, who was sitting on a stool in his cell to say his office, suddenly exclaimed: "I have come under the shadow of a great fear; I am very much afraid. Read me the Recommendation for a Passing Soul, and say it so loudly that I may hear it." This Palóu did, assisted by the Carmel priest and by a number of soldiers and neophytes who had come into the room. Serra himself made all the responses in the prayers, still sitting upon the stool. At the end the dying man cried: "Thanks be to God! Thanks be to God! He has quite taken away my fear." This being over, Serra sat in the chair by his table and quietly completed the reading of his office.

When he had finished, Palóu suggested that, as it was now afternoon, Serra take a little broth, and after Serra had done so, he said: "Now let us go to rest." The officers from the presidio and those of a ship that happened to be in the harbor tiptoed out; they knew that Serra was dying and they wished to be where they could be quickly summoned, so they dined at the mission. When Palóu came later in the afternoon into his friend's cell, he found him apparently sleeping. But it was not sleep but death. It was the Feast of St. Augustine, August 28, 1774.

V: John Carroll

(1735–1815)

John Carroll was to become the first Bishop of Baltimore, and then the first Archbishop, with jurisdiction over the entire United States, as it was at the time of the founding of the republic. It is to be remembered that, as a corollary of political independence, went a guarantee, under the federal Constitution, of religious liberty.

Catholics in the new nation numbered at most 30,000, and were ministered to by only twenty-four priests. Moreover, those priests were nearly all rather old and infirm, and, as they all had been Jesuits, the suppression of the Society in 1773 by Pope Clement XIV struck them a severe blow, with no chance, so far as anybody could foresee, of recovery. Secularized, they continued to work among their scattered flocks, but under increasing difficulties. Had it not been for the return from abroad of John Carroll, a very able and vigorous and relatively young priest, driven back to his native Maryland by the suppression, the situation of Catholics in the United States would have been perilous in spite of the new spirit animating the country.

In several of the colonies the practice of the Catholic religion was absolutely prohibited, with the inevitable result that such Catholics who went there—commonly as indentured servants, who had no choice in the matter—were lost to the Church, however stubbornly they had for a while clung to their faith. Indeed, it may be said that prior to the Revolution only in Pennsylvania, where about 6,000 Catholics were to be found, were they relatively free. But in Maryland, where most of the remaining number lived—elsewhere, as in Virginia and the Carolinas, they were the merest sprinkling—they existed only under severe disabilities.

The Catholics of Maryland had, however, one considerable advantage. Their colony had been founded under a charter given to Lord Baltimore by King James I. While this made no provision for religious liberty, Baltimore, as proprietor, was able to see to it that all who settled in his colony—Protestants and Catholics alike—should not have their conscience molested. His was in no sense a specifically Catholic undertaking, and such priests who went to Maryland did so on exactly the same footing as the other "gentlemen adventurers"—that is, they had to support themselves as planters while being free to minister to the spiritual needs of Catholics. Lord Baltimore had, in fact, to be extremely circumspect in all that he did; so much was this the case that it was even given out that the name Maryland adopted by his colony was really in honor of Henrietta Maria, wife of Charles I, who had succeeded his father in 1625.

Even such prudent safeguards soon proved ineffective, for Protestants became dominant in the Maryland Assembly, and after the establishment of the Commonwealth in England, following the execution of Charles I in 1649, Virginia invaded the colony to the north, defeated its governor on March 24, 1655, abrogated the palatine charter and proscribed all practice of Catholicism. From then on Catholics were permitted to exist only under sufferance, unable publicly to hold services, with all power to maintain a school withdrawn, disbarred from office, and subject to discriminatory taxation. For them the winning of American independence, as it brought with it religious toleration, may be said to have been paradise regained.

This happy issue—not only for Lord Baltimore's old colony but for the United States—was to a considerable extent furthered by the family of John Carroll, in particular by his brother Daniel, who was one of the signers of the Constitution, and by his cousin, Charles Carroll of Carrollton, who had signed the Declaration of Independence. Maryland had a number of Catholics who enjoyed a solid, if modest, prosperity, and a few, such as the Carrolls, who were exactly of the same social class as the great gentlemen of Virginia, with whom in fact they had friendly and cordial contacts.

John Carroll had left Maryland in 1748 with his cousin Charles Carroll of Carrollton to enter the famous Jesuit College of St. Omer, in the northwest corner of France. After completing his studies there, Charles went on to study law at Paris and London, before returning to America in 1765. John, however, joined the Jesuits soon after he arrived in France, and in due course became a professor at their college at Liège, remaining in this position except for a short period when he acted as traveling tutor to the son of Lord Stoughton.

He returned to America at just the right moment. In October, 1774, the Continental Congress drew up three quite different addresses about the Quebec Act. The provisions of that act not only gave religious freedom to Canada, but extended that territory's operations to the Ohio and the Mississippi, at the same time prohibiting American colonists, at least for the time being, from settling beyond the Appalachians. The first of these protests, dated October 21, 1774, expressed astonishment that Parliament sought to establish in Canada a religion "fraught with sanguinary and impious concepts." Five days later, the Canadians were sent an assurance of American liberality and an invitation of amity. Yet that very day a petition of protest was sent to the King for "extending the limits of Quebec, abolishing the English and restoring the French laws, whereby great numbers of English freemen are subjected to the latter, and establishing an absolute government and the Roman Catholic religion throughout those vast regions, that border on the westerly and northerly boundaries of the free Protestant English settlements." In all this there was not only double-dealing but a suppression of the fact that under the Quebec Act Protestants were expressly exempt from the payment of tithes to the Catholic clergy.

It is hardly to be wondered at that the French Canadians turned a deaf ear to the appeal that the Continental Congress had made, and held Americans in contempt. Had the matter been handled in a straightforward fashion, it might have been possible to have brought Canada in on the side of the colonies. Instead, as the address to the Canadians failed of its purpose, a military expedition under Benedict Arnold was sent across the St. Lawrence. That sort of persuasion also met with no success, and a mission was finally sent to Canada, something that should have been done at the outset. However, it was too late; the Canadians remembered the clear language of October, 1774.

The better American minds were, of course, free from such sentiments. George Washington issued a proclamation discountenancing the celebration of "Pope's Day," the name under which the Fifth of November—Guy Fawkes' Day—was known in America; Congress even attended a Mass in Philadelphia for the repose of the soul of the Spanish ambassador. But while Spain and France appreciated the courtesy, the incensed Canadians were not to be placated. Bishop Briand of Quebec let it be known that he intended to honor the oath of allegiance he had taken to George III.

The commission finally sent to Canada was composed of three very able men—Benjamin Franklin, Samuel Chase, and Charles Carroll of Carrollton. Fr. John Carroll was asked to accompany them, not in an official but an advisory capacity. It was rightly thought that a Catholic priest should be with them to put the aims of the Americans in their true light. That both of the Carrolls, having been educated in France, spoke French fluently was also regarded as a great advantage.

If the commission failed to win over the Canadians, there were some other unlooked for and later results. A definite offer was made to Charles Carroll that he go to France as American Ambassador. He wisely refused, however, writing to Washington: "I am the one man who must be kept entirely in the background." Understanding the anti-Catholic prejudices of many Americans, he realized that he would be doing his co-religionists a distinct disservice. He preferred to serve his own state rather than to be a member of the Continental Congress and later even refused the seat of senator at Washington. Yet he did enough by signing the Declaration of Independence, and it was he, perhaps more than any other man, who saved George Washington when a cabal was forming against him during the dark days of Valley Forge.

He probably would have refused to run as Federalist candidate for the presidency in 1792, though the party wished to have him. As to this, however, speculation is useless, for the offer was not explicity made, as Washington, at the last minute and rather reluctantly decided to seek a second term. But it is interesting to note that in those early days of the republic Charles Carroll's Catholicism was not thought to disbar him from the highest office his country had to offer. Only later did such an illiberal consideration enter the minds of some Americans.

It would not be out of place here to mention the "Address of the Catholics" to George Washington in 1790, which was probably written by John Carroll and signed by him as well as by Charles Carroll of Carrollton, Daniel Carroll, Dominic Lynch of New York and Thomas Fitzsimmons of Philadelphia. Other denominations wrote somewhat similar addresses and, of course, all received the President's courteous thanks. To the Catholics he wrote in a most warm way on March 12, 1790, saying, among other things: "I presume that your fellow citizens will not forget the patriotic part which you took in the accomplishment of their Revolution, and the establishment of their Government—or the important assistance which they received from a nation in which the Roman Catholic faith is professed."

American Catholics have always been proud of this reply from Washington, and they well understood that the President meant his words to reach the rest of Americans. Nobody knew better than Washington that American Catholics had contributed towards the winning of Independence at least as much, in proportion to the numbers, as any other religious denomination. Moylan and Thomas Fitzsimmons had been secretaries of his and had distinguished themselves as officers in the field, and John Barry, though his opportunities were limited, has a right to be regarded as the "father of the American Navy." In addition, there were invaluable services rendered to the American cause by the Carrolls and other Marylanders in the field of statesmanship. As John Carroll soberly put it: "They concurred with perhaps greater unanimity than any other body of men in recommending and promoting that government from whose influence America anticipates all the blessings of justice, peace, plenty, good order, and civil and religious liberty."

But this, of course, was said many years later. We must return to the unsuccessful mission of Franklin, Chase and Charles Carroll to Canada. It was at this time that Fr. Carroll, who accompanied the commissioners at the request of Congress, won the good opinion of Franklin. The priest went out of his way to be agreeable to that charming old sceptic, not because he thought of any benefits that he might derive, but because he liked Franklin and because the elderly gentleman needed the attentions he could supply. In turn, Franklin held Carroll in the highest esteem.

John Carroll, from the time of his arrival in America in 1774, almost at once became the leader of the clergy. He had no position of authority among them, but his relative youth and his ability and his energy established an unconscious ascendency. In 1784 he was named superior of the American missions, and was given the right to confer confirmation. On February 27, 1785, he accepted the position of prefect apostolic, in which he had additional powers of a bishop, without actually being one.

A prefect apostolic helped a good deal in the administration of ecclesiastical affairs, but a bishop was really needed. Though this was very evident to the American clergy, most of them were afraid of what might happen should a bishop appear among them. Not until the Episcopalians ventured to elect one of their clergy to be sent to England for consecration were American Catholics emboldened to do the same.

The Holy See then gave the American clergy the privilege —but for that occasion only—of electing the man they wanted appointed. This was to remove the possibility of there being any criticism by the American public, such as might have occurred had there been direct papal action. The outcome of the election was a foregone conclusion, for there was only one priest in the United States who possessed the requisite qualifications; the only vote cast against John Carroll was his own.

He went to England for his consecration, as he had given his friend Charles Plowden a promise that he would do so, for it had been recognized for some years that when the United States received its first bishop it would be Carroll. Quite apart from his promise, he would undoubtedly have gone to England, rather than to Quebec or Mexico or Puerto Rico, because only there could he promote other projects that he had in mind. Donations towards the founding of a college at Georgetown might have come from other countries, but the college would need a president, and Carroll realized that he ought to be an English-speaking priest. By discussing the whole question with Plowden, Carroll hoped that Plowden himself might accept the position.

In this he did not succeed. Nor did he succeed—at least not in the way he had envisaged—in obtaining in England recruits for the mission in America, which it was now his responsibility to build up. Very few young Americans were presenting themselves for the priesthood, yet the need for priests had greatly increased, due to the number of new immigrants. Even had Carroll been able to obtain recruits in America, the nearest seminary to which he could send them was that in Montreal, and Americans were not likely to receive a very cordial reception there or to remain long even if they were admitted.

Though John Carroll did not succeed in finding any English priests willing to go to the United States—for England needed the few priests it had—something happened which in the long-run proved even better: Jean-Jacques Emery, Superior-General of the Sulpicians in Paris, came forward with offers of help. Though Bishop Carroll had so little enthusiasm over the prospect of staffing his churches with Frenchmen that he even declined Emery's invitation that he go to Paris to see him, Emery, not to be put down, sent one of his own men over to England to see Carroll.

The offer made was one that Carroll was in no position to refuse. The Sulpicians undertook to erect their own seminary in Baltimore and to send not only a faculty but seminarians. Moreover, they said that they would lend some of their men to teach at the projected college at Georgetown. Though Carroll still would have much preferred an English-speaking clergy, as these were evidently not to be obtained just then he could make good use of French priests and any young men they trained in their seminary.

Great things were to come from this seminary, though the seminarians the Sulpicians brought with them from France were few, and Americans at first did not show themselves very eager to prepare for the priesthood under Frenchmen. This being the case, and as the college at Georgetown did not attract many students during the first years, there was not enough work at either place for the Sulpicians that Père

Emery had sent to the United States. From one point of view this was fortunate, because Carroll was able to send several of them as missionaries in the west, and though the managing of seminaries was the distinctive Sulpician vocation, as missionaries the Sulpicians gave most devoted service. Emery, however, who was naturally thinking about his seminary in Baltimore, and was greatly disappointed at the results obtained there, planned to recall his men to France. Had he done so, it would have been disastrous for the Church in the United States. Fortunately, Pope Pius VII, who was in Paris in 1804 for the coronation of the Emperor Napoleon, begged Emery not to abandon an enterprise that America so badly needed. Only this direct intervention saved the Baltimore seminary.

Though this seminary was Carroll's main hope for the future, he did obtain recruits from priests—mostly from Ireland or Germany—who came to the United States, often because they were problems in their native land. However, they bore letters of recommendation from their bishops, and Carroll hardly had any choice but to accept them and to send them to one of the many places under his jurisdiction where there was crying need for a priest.

Several of these men were valuable acquisitions. Others continued to be problems and, under existing circumstances, were not easy to control. In one instance, control was so resented that the priest returned to the land of his birth to publish a pamphlet accusing Bishop Carroll of a surreptitious attempt to revive the suppressed Society of Jesus in the United States, a charge which, though entirely without foundation, might have had a damaging effect. It was impossible for Carroll to issue a public rejoinder, as that undoubtedly would have involved him in acrimonious controversy; all he could do was to write privately to the priest's original bishop and count upon him to make the truth of the matter known.

Then, too, there were chaplains with the French forces during the War of Independence who either remained here after those forces left or who found America so much to their liking as to return soon afterwards. And there were several instances of Dominican or Franciscan friars coming to this country. In some cases men of considerable ability (but also of undue ambition) believed that they would advance more rapidly in America.

Some trouble also sprang out of the trustee system, and John Carroll has sometimes been blamed for permitting it to come into existence. Yet he really had little choice about it, for ecclesiastical property, under existing secular law, could be held only in the name of a committee elected by the individual churches. Trusteeism would have been harmless enough had all the trustees devoted themselves to the good of the congregation of which they were the representatives, instead of intruding themselves into concerns that were none of their business. Here the trustees themselves were sometimes less to blame than a few clerics from abroad who used them to build up a personal party. These clerics told the lay trustees about the *jus patronatus* which existed in some European countries, and this the trustees, in their ignorance of canon law, interpreted to mean that they had the right to appoint and discharge their own pastors. Actually, they had no such power; still less did trustees have any right to withholding a priest's salary. Yet when, as sometimes happened, they carried the case into a civil court, they were upheld, because the state laws had been drawn up by men acquainted only with the Protestant system. However, to take legal action against their bishop was in such downright violation of canon law that they made themselves liable to excommunication.

Some years after Carroll's death, Archbishop Hughes of New York, while suggesting that Carroll had introduced trusteeism, gave him a kind of exculpation by adding that this was because Carroll "wished to assimilate, as far as possible, the administration of Catholic Church property in a way that would harmonize with the democratic principles on which the new government was founded." This no doubt did motivate Carroll. He was also a mild and moderate man who was by nature disposed to hope for the good of which the system was possible, and at the same time was likely to ignore the unjustifiable ways in which it was capable of being used. But the primary fact was that the system was really part of Protestantism and did not belong in Catholicism, except to the extent that a board of trustees could be serviceable to the pastor if it restricted itself to the temporalities of the congregation.

Some of the German clerics who arrived in this country were almost more troublesome. They began to demand that a bishop of their own stock be appointed to govern them; one priest meanwhile going into schism, and his congregation assembling with muskets in their hands to keep Carroll out. This man—Caesarius Reuter—had previously gone to Rome to complain that Carroll had threatened to excommunicate any priest who preached in German, which was a palpable lie, as there were German sermons in twelve of the churches under Carroll's jurisdiction. In the end the bishop carried the case before the secular courts, which ruled in May, 1805, that he was the bishop of all nationalities.

Coping with difficulties of the kind that have been indicated, but far more often meeting with no distressing obstacles, Carroll as prefect-apostolic and then as bishop saw the Catholic Church in the United States steadily expand. In 1799 he obtained a coadjutor in Leonard Neale, and in 1808 a division of his immense diocese was brought about, the dioceses of Philadelphia, New York and Boston being erected, with another, which ran from the southern boundary of Tennessee to the Great lakes and west as far as the Mississippi.

When the Louisiana Purchase was completed Carroll also became administrator of the new territories. It did not involve much additional work, as priests there were few, except around New Orleans.

Though as prefect-apostolic, bishop and, since 1808, as Archbishop of Baltimore, John Carroll had had many difficulties to overcome, and though trusteeism remained to harass the American hierarchy for many years, it must be said that his administration—wise, good-humored, tolerant but firm—has a record of unbroken advance. Not of himself but of the American Constitution could he boast to Charles Plowden on February 28, 1799, that he saw in the improved situation in England something that was due to the American example. Emancipation in that country was still thirty years away, but a steady progress was being made towards it, despite the bitterness with which it was assailed. "I cannot help thinking," Carroll told Plowden, "that you are indebted to America for this piece of service."

A tangible mark of Catholic growth was the erection of the cathedral in Baltimore, which Carroll did not live to see completed, but which still is in use as a cathedral, though a larger structure is to replace it in another part of the city. B. H. Latrobe's simple and charming design was for a long time—indeed, until the building of the new St. Patrick's Cathedral in New York—the finest ecclesiastical building in the United States, and even now is among the finest in its quiet, dignified way. One of the means by which funds were raised for building it was a lottery. It is rather amusing to record that when the drawing was made the archbishop (of all people) won the first prize. This he immediately put back into the pool, so that there had to be a second drawing.

On December 3, 1815, John Carroll died at Baltimore, nearly eighty-one years old. He and his friend George Washington have often been compared, and there were in truth many resemblances between the two men, both of whom were great gentlemen, patient, sagacious and statesmanlike. He was like Washington in his moderation and tolerance and persistence in the face of what often seemed to be insurmountable difficulties. It was extremely fortunate that the guidance of Church and State in this country should, during the critical formative years have been in the hands of these two men.

VI: Pierre Toussaint

(1755–1853)

Philip Schuyler, a descendant of the general of that name, and of Alexander Hamilton, whose wife projected the biography written by Mrs. Lee, who used her notes, once remarked: "I have known Christians who were not gentlemen, gentlemen who were not Christians, but one man I know who is both—and that man is black." People found that this tall dignified Negro was to be trusted with any confidence. Both his dignity and his trustworthiness were remarkable in one whose gay ebullience of temperament was sometimes exhibited in a dance or a song. He was also what Christians and gentlemen should be, but rarely are—saintly. For that reason, and because the saintliness appeared in circumstances in which one would hardly expect to find it, this chapter about him is being written.

Pierre Toussaint was born a slave in San Domingo in 1755, and belonged to an admirable couple named Bérard, who treated him less as a slave than as a member of the family. This was at the time the majority of slave owners there treated their property in human flesh with an oppressive cruelty, whose limits were dictated only by the practical conclusion that it was not to their own interest to subject their slaves to such ill usage as might diminish their value. It was this cruelty that led to their subsequent uprising and a massacre of the whites.

From his grandmother Toussaint had learned to read and write—though merely the simplest elements; but his master, noticing his intelligence and intellectual curiosity, gave him the free run of his library, thereby sharpening his wits and increasing his slave's refinement of feeling. Vastly more important was the affectionate esteem in which he was held by all the Bérards. A son and daughter by his master's first marriage were his godparents at baptism, and though they went to France, so that he never saw them again, we know from the letters he received from them that they held him in close love and respect.

Of such a family Toussaint had not the slightest particle of fear. They brought him up with careful attention to his religious training, and though his piety exceeded even theirs, it was their great merit that they had put Pierre on the road to sanctity.

At the outbreak of the French Revolution, the Assembly in Paris voted that slaves in the French possessions should be free. But the two mulattos who carried the news to San Domingo were seized by the planters and broken upon the wheel in the public square; other Negroes who dared to claim their freedom were hanged. The result might have been foreseen: under Dessalines and Henri Christophe the slaves rose in rebellion. Christophe, who proclaimed himself king, and was a leader of an energy and ability that equaled his cruelty, won for Santo Domingo an independence that lasted until 1820, when he committed suicide. In 1801, however, Toussaint l'Ouverture, the wisest and most moderate of the Negro leaders, was captured by the expedition sent against the island by Napoleon. He was imprisoned in France, where "as the most unhappy man of men," he was the subject of one of Wordsworth's sonnets.

During the upheaval many of the whites got away safely, among them the Bérards, who took with them some of their faithful slaves, not only Pierre and his sister, but the child whom he was eventually to marry. It was expected that the troubles would die down before long and that the refugees would return. The fugitives went to many different places, but the Bérards and their entourage settled in New York City, where they found a house near St. Peter's in Barclay Street, at that time the only Catholic church in the city. It had been founded largely through the instrumentality of Hector St. John de Crèvecoeur, author of the *Letters of an American Farmer*. During the sixty years during which Toussaint lived in New York he attended the six o'clock Mass at this church, and was never known to be absent except during his last illness, when he was close to being a centenarian.

The Bérards had left San Domingo in 1787. Four years later during a lull in the storm, Monsieur Bérard returned to the island, only to die there. He had not succeeded in salvaging much of his holdings, but his slaves continued to serve his widow, now in straitened circumstances. It was fortunate for her that Pierre had been apprenticed to the leading hairdresser in New York and that he became so highly skilled that, when his indentures ran out, he was able to set up in business for himself. Though he was still a slave, he obtained the patronage of most of the wealthy families of New York. In time he became the sole support of his mistress, yet also was able to set aside enough money to purchase by degrees the manumission of his sister and the young woman, Juliette Noel, whom he married when he was fifty-six. These were not the only slaves he helped to release from servitude; it never seems to have occurred to him to purchase his own freedom, great as was the store he set upon it. He received this as a free gift from Madame Bérard in 1809, when she was dying and he was in late middle life.

Bérard's daughter Marie had married a young man named Gabriel Nicholas, and she and her husband continued to live at the house on Reade Street, where Pierre Toussaint and his sister and Juliette were installed on the top floor. Nicholas, like all the refugees from San Domingo, was virtually destitute, except for a somewhat precarious livelihood he earned by playing in a theatre orchestra. Presumably he was able to contribute something to the support of his wife and mother-in-law, yet even after Toussaint was free he remained the main support of Marie.

While he had been working hard as a hairdresser, he bought most of the family's food and supplied most of the requirements of Madame Bérard, that she might continue to surround herself with something like the luxury to which she had been accustomed. And after he married Juliette, he had her cook a delicious dinner every day for a poor French nobleman, whose pride might have refused this charity had he ever discovered that the food came from former slaves and not from one of his artistocratic friends whom he supposed to be his secret benefactors. This amused the vivacious Juliette a great deal, nor was the humor of the situation lost upon Pierre himself, who strictly forbade her to let the truth out.

There were, however, charities that it was impossible to conceal, in addition to many that were never publicized. For instance, when in 1841 the Bishop of Nancy, preaching in New York, remarked that the French colony there seemed to show so little concern for their salvation that they did not establish their own church, it was the ex-slave Pierre Toussaint who sent the first donation of $100 towards what became St. Vincent de Paul's Church, to be located on Canal Street. And when Bishop Hughes brought a group of Sisters from Emmitsburg to found a diocesan orphanage, reconstituting the Sisters as a new branch directly under the ordinary, Toussaint brought them every month what he was able to give himself or had collected from his wealthy customers, all of whom became his personal friends.

At that time fashionable ladies went in for elaborate coiffures which had to be frequently built up anew. These ladies looked forward to the visits of their Negro hairdresser, always so wise in advice and so kindhearted. Best of all, he was unfailingly tactful and discreet; they could tell him anything, certain that it would go no further. Among his distinguished customers were the Schuylers, the Livingstons, the Hamiltons, the Hosacks, the La Farges and the Binsses. People in the street often stared with astonishment to see a great lady stop her carriage, to take the hand of the old Negro in both her own.

This constituted something not only remarkable, but unique. Pierre lived into the days when abolitionist agitation created a great deal of animosity, even in the North. And in the South the memory of what had happened in San Domingo aroused some fears there that the Negroes in the United States might rise against their masters. But Toussaint was untouched by it all; because of his character he was held in profound respect.

He was, indeed, known to be not only a very good but a very charitable man, and many of the rich ladies who employed him made him their almoner—not because he directly asked them for contributions, but because they had happened to discover some of the many kind acts that he performed. In old age, when a friend said: "Toussaint, you are now well off; why do you not retire?" the answer came: "In that case, Madame, I should not have enough for others." In addition to his gifts of money, he acted as a kind of employment agent for those in need of work, giving his time without thinking of any return.

Toussaint confessed to having a very quick temper—but the gentle St. Francis de Sales also used to say this of himself. But nobody observed in either of these men anything but the sweetest affability, courtesy and tact. Thus, when a Catholic friend was a guest of the Schuylers, she asked him whether he would give her a place in his pew at St. Peter's when she went to Mass on Sunday. He promised that she would be accommodated, but, when she arrived, Pierre showed her into the pew of a man whom he knew to be away. "But I expected that you would let me sit in your pew!"

she exclaimed, only to get the answer: "No, madame, that would not be fitting."

Only rarely did anything like an ugly incident occur. The worst of these was when a new usher at the old St. Patrick's Cathedral on Mott Street, a young man who did not know to whom he was speaking, made some insulting remark to the venerable Negro. The trustees of St. Patrick's were greatly incensed when they heard what had happened, and their president, Louis F. Binsse, wrote a letter of apology on their behalf, saying that the usher was very repentant after having been severely reprimanded, adding: "Everybody knows, my dear Toussaint, that if God by His will has created you as well as your good wife with a black skin, by His grace He has made your hearts and souls as white as snow."

Mrs. Hannah Lee, the first of Toussaint's biographers, quotes several letters from the Bérards who had settled in France which show that, though they had not seen Toussaint for many years, they continued to hold him in the most affectionate esteem. An unnamed friend wrote when Toussaint was on his death bed that while Juliette, who had died in 1851, was a very good woman, she was not the match of her husband. "I never met with any other of his race," this friend went on, "who made me forget his color. Toussaint, for his deportment, discretion, good sense and entire trustworthiness and fidelity, might have discharged creditably all the functions of a courtier or privy councillor." And a Negro friend in Port-au-Prince wrote to Toussaint in 1837: "I have observed many men and observed them closely, but I have never seen one that deserved as you do the name of a religious man. I have always followed your counsels, and now more than ever, for there are few like you. Good men are as rare as a fine day in America."

Similar opinions were held by everyone who knew Pierre Toussaint. After the death of his wife, who was twenty-one years younger than himself, and whom he had married relatively late in life, he was left very lonely, and as he was in his ninety-sixth year, well nigh helpless. Though Juliette was in her seventies when she died, Pierre still thought of her as a child. And Euphemia, his niece and adopted daughter, who had been the delight of his eyes, had died of tuberculosis in 1829. Indeed he would have been helpless except for his close union with God.

He lived by himself in a little house on Franklin Street which he had bought. Always abstemious and careful in the way he handled money, he gave up hairdressing at last and retired; though he had always enjoyed excellent health, when he reached his nineties he no longer had the strength to work. Yet he did not go to bed, not feeling that he was ill, and sat up in his dressing gown to receive the hosts of friends of former days.

Not only had he been able to buy a house, but he had acquired a small competence, quite sufficient for his modest needs—with enough to spare for him to be able to continue his charities. These were not confined to New York. However hard he tried to keep them secret, he was not always able to do so. We know that he and Juliette, as she had relatives in Baltimore, helped to found a school there for Negro children, most of them refugees from San Domingo. This was under the direction of one of the priests from the Sulpician Seminary, and was conducted by the Oblate Sisters of Providence—at the start a group of only four, who constituted the first community of Negro women in this country.

Though so far as we know Toussaint confined his charities to the United States, he had keen interest in charitable activities in all parts of the world. Thus Alfred de Lagnel, then secretary to Hyde de Neuville, who had formerly been the French Ambassador at Washington, wrote to him from Paris about Cardinal Cheverus, who had been the first Bishop of Boston. Alfred's letter to Toussaint read in part: "We will have here for some weeks longer the venerable M. de Cheverus, formerly Bishop of Boston, now Archbishop of Bordeaux, and who has just been raised to the rank of cardinal. This holy man, worthy prince of the Church, is always the same, a living image of the Apostles in simplicity and self-abnegation. I have met him in the streets of Bordeaux, having under his arm a package of clothing which he was carrying to the poor." He and the Negro who had been a slave somehow strike one as having been cast in the same mould.

Mrs. Lee gave an account of her last visit to Pierre. She found the old man, who was then close to a hundred, sitting in an arm chair, supported by pillows and wearing his dressing gown. "A more perfect representation of a gentleman," she wrote, "I have seldom seen. His head was strewn with the 'blossoms of the grave.'" They had last met at the funeral of Mrs. Lee's sister, Mary Anne Schuyler; when he spoke of it, he shook with emotion and floods of tears rolled down his cheeks. But he was too weak to talk much. "It is all so changed! so changed!" Within a month his visitors noted that his speech had become low and indistinct, but that he was calm and cheerful, "the expression of his countenance truly religious." Late in June, when Elizabeth Hamilton Schuyler visited him, he said in French: "God is with me," and when asked whether there was anything he wanted he smiled and answered: "Nothing on earth." Four days later, on June 30, 1853, he breathed his last, at ninety-eight years of age.

The pastor of St. Peter's who preached his requiem, climaxed it with the statement: "There are few left among the clergy superior to him in devotion and zeal for the Church and the glory of God; among laymen, none."

VII: Benedict Joseph Flaget

(1763–1850)

The temptation arises of entitling this chapter "Flaget and the Frontier"—except that there were several frontiers. While the Catholic settlers in Kentucky were the first considerable group to cross the Alleghenies, not long afterwards Prince Gallitzin was at work among the mountains themselves, and only a little later Samuel Mazzuchelli traveled the midwest and Peter De Smet the Rocky Mountains. Their success is due in part to the fact that it was Flaget who created their opportunity.

When the Louisiana Purchase was made, the new area was administered by Archbishop Carroll until his death in 1815, and this meant that (except for the district around New Orleans) the only priests who went into the enormous tract which doubled the size of the United States were those under Flaget's jurisdiction. Even Dubourg's diocese of "Louisiana and the Floridas" may be though of as within Flaget's "Frontier," as well as the dioceses of Cincinnati and Vincennes, which were carved out of Flaget's immense diocese of Bardstown.

Though Benedict Joseph Flaget had worked from 1892 to 1895 in Indiana, he had not been the first priest to go there. Rivet, a Frenchman from Canada, had worked at the French settlement of Vincennes before him. And Pierre Gibault, vicar-general of Bishop Briand of Quebec, had a good deal to do with the winning of the northwest by the United States, as George Rogers Clark has acknowledged. Yet these priests were there because Vincennes was in English eyes part of Canada until American arms succeeded in wresting it away. When that happened, the statesmanlike Carroll was quick to perceive the importance of the West. As it had begun to fill up with adventurous settlers, many of them Catholics, he recognized that their spiritual needs must be met at once if they were to be saved for the Church. It was for this reason that in 1808 Flaget was nominated for Bardstown, the first diocese established beyond the Alleghenies.

As early as 1774, white settlers began to arrive in Kentucky. Such of them as were Catholics from Maryland were drawn there because in the state from which they came almost the only crop was tobacco, and this rapidly exhausted the soil; in Kentucky, "dark and bloody ground" though it might be, a wider range was possible, and there the soil so far had been untilled.

The Catholic settlers always came in groups, partly because only when they were in sizeable numbers could they feel safe from the Indians. But they had an additional motive: by forming themselves into colonies, they could more easily be ministered to by a priest—when a priest should arrive. These Catholic colonies, in north-central Kentucky, were nearly all in a rough oval about sixty-five miles long and forty wide. A few settlements were made on the Ohio River, but none of them was very far away. The first church—as distinguished from the "stations" in farmhouses that had had to serve as churches—was built in Jefferson County in 1811.

The first priest who went to Kentucky—except for such occasional visits as had been made from those laboring in Indiana—was the Capuchin Fr. Whelan. Insufficient provision was made for his support, and he soon departed. Stephen Theodore Badin went out in 1793. He was the first to be ordained priest at the Baltimore Seminary, and had come to the United States with the first Sulpicians. An extremely able and energetic man, he was also something of a rigorist. This, unfortunately, did not extend to his own behavior where business matters were concerned, and Flaget at one time was on the point of suspending him.

The Belgian Charles Nerinckx, with whose name Badin will always be associated, came to Kentucky in 1804. He also was a rigorist, but there was never a more devoted missionary, nor were there many men who were his equal in courage and strength. One whole night he sat his horse holding off a pack of wolves. One morning he was accosted by a hulking fellow, who proposed to give him a thrashing. Nerinckx quickly threw him on his back and held him there until he acknowledged himself vanquished. Anyone who had seen the ease with which he could handle a heavy log of wood would never have hurled such a challenge.

The rigorism of these two men is strikingly seen in their ban on dancing. And as dancing was one of the very few amusements available in Kentucky, this fell very hard upon the people. Badin often declared that he had no objection to dancing as such, only it had to be under conditions which it was rarely possible to meet. We must remember that in France and some adjoining countries there was a kind of "hangover" from Jansenism. Its positive doctrinal errors had, it is true, disappeared, but its puritanical spirit—still to be encountered among some Catholics—continued to exist.

The Dominicans, who arrived in Kentucky the same year that Nerinckx did—led by the Marylander Edgar Fenwick who seventeen years later became the first Bishop of Cincinnati—said quite bluntly that Nerinckx and Badin were Jansenistically inclined. They retorted that the Dominicans were lax in their notions, and relations between the friars and the other missionaries became somewhat strained, especially as the people naturally took shelter under the Dominicans' views. And as these friars were Marylanders (except for a sprinkling of Englishmen), they sympathized with the Catholics of Kentucky, who, like themselves, had come from Maryland.

When Flaget was made Bishop of Bardstown in 1808, with

a diocese that extended from the southern boundary of Tennessee to the Great Lakes, and from Pennsylvania, Maryland, Virginia, and South Carolina in the East to the Mississippi in the West, it was a tract three times as large as the whole of France. There is no wonder that Flaget, who since 1795 had been working in the Baltimore diocese, during which time he had been on the faculty at Georgetown and then at St. Mary's Seminary, was appalled when he heard of his appointment. In great distress he appealed to John Carroll, just made the metropolitan, assuring him that he had prayed much about the question before asking to be spared a burden to which he felt himself quite unequal. That brought from Carroll the smiling retort: "Don't you think that I have prayed about it, too?"

Flaget then went to see Jacques-André Emery, Superior-General of the Sulpicians, to which society Flaget belonged. Emery had sent the Sulpicians to Baltimore in 1784; but twenty years later had nearly withdrawn them because he was disappointed in what they had, up to that time, accomplished in America. He gave short shrift to Flaget, to whom his first words were: "Monseigneur, why are you not in your diocese?" All the comfort the poor bishop-elect got from that source was a sewing kit and a cook book. The first no doubt proved handy, but one may wonder what use was found in the cook book by a man who used to say wryly that a missionary on the frontier must be prepared to live upon nothing—and to cook it himself.

Flaget was always inclined to stress the hardships of missionary life, because he well realized that they would make a powerful appeal to the type of man he wished to obtain. He himself had the roughest kind of shack as his episcopal "palace" and, though a bishop, spent a large part of every day in the saddle. Had he not taken as his motto *In Coelo requies?* There was no need for rest upon earth, as he would have eternity for that. The regimen proved to be good for him, for he was going on ninety when he died.

It is remarkable how many of the Sulpicians, an institute founded for the sole purpose of conducting seminaries, should have become missionaries. The explanation is, partly, that in the United States there was not enough work at the Baltimore seminary or the college at Georgetown to keep all of them fully occupied. They were too zealous to be idle when so much needed to be done. They started a college at Baltimore, which was later absorbed by the seminary, and another college, Mount St. Mary's, at Emmitsburg, Maryland. When the Sulpicians at Baltimore after a while refused to accept financial responsibility for the second of these, its founder Jean Dubois and his second-in-command, Simon Bruté, regretfully severed themselves from the Society.

Both men eventually became bishops, as did several others: Dubourg, David, and Chabrat. Marechal and Eccleston were, in turn, Archbishops of Baltimore. Gabriel Richard, who did not become a bishop, was the only Catholic priest ever elected to Congress, edited what is sometimes considered the first American Catholic paper, and served as vice-president of what became the University of Michigan. Of the eight first bishops who were, or had been, Sulpicians during his life, Flaget was the first to be appointed.

During the early days of Kentucky the amenities of civilization hardly existed, though by the time Flaget went there in 1808 conditions had considerably improved. The log cabins were more commodious and some had been replaced by frame houses. Most people still had to work from sunrise to sunset, for not much extensive farming could be done until the ground was cleared of trees. The people were highly sociable, whenever they got the chance; even the shucking of corn became the occasion for a gathering of neighbors. If the work were of a heavier kind (and sometimes when it was light) in all likelihood there was some quaffing of the corn whiskey that could be made so cheaply. Though this might now and then be to excess, upon the whole it could be said that these Catholics of the frontier were excellent people, simple, frugal and innocent. And they were so devout that, in the absence of a priest (and as those working among them had twenty-four stations to visit, saying Mass on Sundays at two that were ten miles apart, it was never more than once a month that anybody could be present at Mass), the people assembled in their station, and one of their number would read aloud the Mass prayers, except those of the Consecration. To visit the sick a priest often had to ride twenty miles.

The zeal of the people was really exemplary. They kept a very strict Lent, and whenever possible a retreat was given to a prospective bride and groom before marriage. The rule about Mass attendance was that, if one could ride, one was expected to be present, provided that the distance between one's home and the station was not more than ten miles; if one had to walk, the radius was shortened to five. Most carried their shoes in their hands and put them on only upon reaching the station, unless the weather was cold.

Usually, the station was only one of the larger and more centrally located log cabins, but sometimes a town hall or a Protestant meeting house could be borrowed. A corps of catechists, both men and women, was organized, and there were a number of pious societies, and every Catholic belonged to at least one of which.

In general, relations between Catholics and Protestants were friendly. But bigots did show themselves now and then, and one minister gave a lecture on confession, asserting that it was always paid for. A Catholic priest who had made a point of being present stood up at the conclusion and asked the audience whether he would have to wear the tattered clothes he had on if even fourpence apiece were paid by his penitents. He was applauded and some of the people in the audience—all non-Catholics—gave him a new suit the next day.

Sometimes the apparent friendliness had a dubious character. Thus, a man who had a large number of lots to sell offered to give a couple of them for the erection of a Catholic church. Judge Webb, the author of *Catholicity in Kentucky,* bluntly told him that Bishop Flaget was not such a fool as to accept; he saw what the motive was. If a church were built, the owner of the other lots would be able to dispose of them at a good price to Catholics who would be sure to want to settle nearby. Yet, there was no animosity in this; merely the parading of good will as a smart business device. The judge considered the motive honorable when a Protestant gave land upon which Catholics might build a school; the latter would then be able to send his children there, as there was no other school within easy reach.

The zealous Nerinckx was very energetic in furthering the establishment of communities of Sisters, being the founder of the Friends of Mary at the Foot of the Cross, otherwise known as the Loretto Sisters—the first religious Institute of American origin, one which still flourishes. He even projected a Negro branch of this order for teaching neglected slaves. But here he was running too far ahead and tilting against Kentucky prejudices. Therefore, though some young colored women actually presented themselves for admission, Bishop Flaget had to intervene to tell Nerinckx that the scheme was not yet practicable.

John-Baptist David, who became Flaget's coadjutor in 1817, was instrumental in founding the Sisters of Charity of Nazareth. They differentiated themselves from those of Emmitsburg because the rule of St. Vincent de Paul did not seem quite suitable for frontier conditions. Dominican Sisters also arrived, as was to be expected, since Dominican priests had preceded them; and the Jesuits of St. Louis sent some of their men to establish St. Mary's College in 1835. However, before long they transferred themselves to New York City where they took charge of the St. John's College which was the nucleus of the future Fordham University.

Soon after his arrival at Bardstown, Flaget established his own seminary—a very primitive kind of building, though not more so than the episcopal palace—and the seminarians had to do much of the housework as well as look after the farm. However, in Martin J. Spalding, Flaget had obtained a man with a high reputation for learning, and who had completed his theological studies in Rome. He was to become his third coadjutor and later, Archbishop of Baltimore.

The cathedral Flaget built was so large a building that he often felt inclined to apologize for being so ostentatious. But his coadjutor, Bishop David, told him that for the building of a small cathedral contributions would be small, whereas for one of what was considered of sufficient splendor the contributions would be very much larger. It was not that much money was available, but there were contributions of limestone and lumber and of free service from artisans. What resulted was a very imposing church, though it is now only that of a parish, as the see had to be transferred in 1841 to the larger city of Louisville. Flaget resigned in 1832, but was persuaded to resume his office the following year, and kept steadily at work until his death in 1850.

Of the other bishops appointed to dioceses on the frontier, two at least deserve some special mention, for they were the kind of men whose personality impressed everybody. One was Simon Gabriel Bruté, who was sent to Vincennes, which had been Flaget's centre of operations when he first went west in 1792.

Prematurely old, and a famous eccentric as well as scholar, Bruté had not been permitted to have his say in the direction of affairs at Mount St. Mary's or during the brief period when he was president of St. Mary's College in Baltimore. Now he accepted a bishopric much against his will, and only because the other bishops in the West whom he had consulted—believing that they would agree with him as to his unfitness—shocked him by unanimously agreeing that he was just the man for the position.

This he decisively proved himself to be, though he still struck many people as being mercurial in temperament and hopelessly unpractical. He even now and then spoke of himself, as his friends in Maryland had done, as "poor crazy Bruté," this despite the fact that, except for some oddities on the surface, his former instability completely disappeared when he became a bishop. He had always been energetic—with his walks of fifty miles in a single day, and his building of totally useless grottoes at Mount St. Mary's—but it was wonderful that the prematurely old man, afflicted with asthma and tuberculosis, and a hernia which might have been expected to make horseback riding impossible, threw himself enthusiastically into building up this new diocese of which he had been put in charge. Before he died, still only sixty, he had founded a seminary and a college, and had gone to France to gather recruits—all within five years.

He had some trouble in getting Mount St. Mary's to return his books, which he had allowed to be used there as the library for its college and seminary. In fact, some of them he never got back, but he managed to salvage 8,000 of them—possibly the largest private library in America at that time. As many are rare volumes, he must have obtained these through the generosity of his brother in France and his own friends, for he was always very poor.

The other bishop of this frontier is William Louis Valentine Dubourg, who was set over the immense diocese of Louisiana and the Floridas in 1815. Unquestionably, he was a very brilliant man, and of a warm, expansive character, though his practical judgment was occasionally erratic. It is to his credit that he brought the Vincentians, the Jesuits, and the Religious of the Sacred Heart to St. Louis.

Benedict Joseph Flaget had had difficulty in scraping up his fare to Bardstown in 1808. Forty years later, his work had so prospered that he had built two cathedrals and consecrated seven bishops, three of whom became Archbishops of Baltimore. Sixty priests were now in his diocese, serving almost as many churches. There were six religious communities; before he died in 1850 there were eight, for the Jesuits came from St. Louis and the Good Shepherd Sisters were about to come. Bardstown had been subdivided no less than eleven times into new dioceses, but even in what remained there were over 35,000 Catholics. It had been a very great work. Not only had Flaget performed his own, but he had prepared for the work that other men were subsequently to do. *In coélo requies.*

VIII: Elizabeth Seton

(1774–1821)

Mother Seton was born two years before the Declaration of Independence was signed. Her father, Richard Bayley, after pursuing his medical studies in England, returned to this country on a British man-of-war and served as a surgeon in the army of General Howe. His sympathies were those of a loyalist, as was equally true of the Seton whose son William married Elizabeth Anne Bayley on January 25, 1794. Yet both men were too highly respected to be made to suffer because of their loyalist sentiments by the triumphant Americans, and Elizabeth Seton, though born technically a British subject, never needed to be naturalized but grew up to be quite definitely an American woman.

Though not wealthy, the Bayleys moved in the best New York society and were related to the Roosevelts. James Roosevelt Bayley was her nephew, and he followed her, after an Amherst education, into the Catholic Church. Nine years after his ordination as a priest he was appointed Bishop of Newark, and in 1872 became Archbishop of Baltimore. He directed that he be buried beside his aunt, and both lie in a kiosk on the grounds of St. Joseph's College, Emmitsburg, with the bodies of several of the Seton daughters or sisters-in-law just outside.

Elizabeth was a lively, charming and good-looking girl, and years later, when advising one of her daughters about social behavior, told her: "When I was young I never found any effect from [dancing] but the most innocent cheerfulness both in public and private. I remember remorse of conscience about so much time lost in it, and my trouble about being so unable to say my prayers—seeing always my partners instead of God—also my vexation at the time it took to prepare dresses for balls." That quaint mingling of religious considerations with those of the *beau monde* is charmingly characteristic.

Her marriage to William Seton was a happy one. She soon became the mother of five children, two sons and three daughters, and her husband prospered in business. Then Seton's health began to decline and, in the hope of regaining it, he and his wife and children went in 1803 at the invitation of his business associates, the Filicchi brothers, to Leghorn in Italy.

When they arrived they were told that, as they had come from New York, where there was an epidemic of yellow fever, they would have to go into quarantine. The lazaretto was several miles from the city and situated on a canal. Though they were assured that it was "the very place for the comfort of the sick," they found it as forbidding as a jail. The room to which they were assigned was desolate, dreary and damp, quite unsuitable for William Seton, who was suffering, indeed dying, from tuberculosis. The big room was so cold that Elizabeth sometimes used her little daughter's skipping rope to keep warm. The former Mary Cooper of Boston, who had married one of the Filicchis, came at once to see them, but could talk to them only across a barrier. However, she sent one of her servants to attend them, and the officials of the lazaretto put up curtains to keep the drafts off William. Two days after Christmas, though at last they had been able to get him out of the lazaretto, he died.

Elizabeth was stricken at the loss, but over and over again her thought ran: "My God, You are my God—how alone I am in the world except for You and my little ones; but You are my Father and doubly theirs." Those who had seen her in the lazaretto had said that, if only she were a Catholic, she would be a saint. They spoke more truly than they knew, for it was during the young widow's stay with the Filicchis—both brothers and their wives being most devout people, and also of considerable intelligence—that Elizabeth felt her first attraction towards Catholicism. The Filicchis made no attempt to argue with her, but she could not avoid being impressed with their way of life, and also with what she had seen in some Catholic churches she had visited. She asked many questions, which they were only too happy to answer.

Of the two brothers Antonio Filicchi was Elizabeth's special friend, and when she was sightseeing in Florence he wrote to her: "Your dear William was the friend of my youth: you are now come in his place. Your soul is even dearer to Antonio, and will be so forever. May the good almighty God enlighten your mind and strengthen your heart to see and follow in religion the surest way to eternal blessings. I shall call for you in Paradise if it is decreed that the vast plains of the ocean shall be betwixt us. Don't discontinue meanwhile to pray, to knock at the door. I am confident that our Redeemer will not be deaf to the humble prayers of so dear a creature." To Antonio more than to anybody else—though both the brothers and their wives had a share in the matter—Elizabeth Seton owed her conversion to the Catholic faith.

Elizabeth was already half a Catholic before she left Italy. When back in New York she opened a small school for the support of her children, and lost little time in getting in touch with Bishop Carroll in Baltimore and Bishop Cheverus in Boston, on the advice of the Filicchis, in the hope that they would clear away a few difficulties that remained. Cheverus wrote to assure her about her "doubts"—really, her hesitancy over making so great a change—"I would therefore advise your joining the Catholic Church as soon as possible, and when doubts arise say only: 'I believe, O Lord; help Thou my unbelief.' "

She had been going to Mass at St. Peter's Church on Barclay Street since Ash Wednesday. Finally, on March 14, 1805, in the presence of Antonio Filicchi (who was on a business trip to the United States) she made her profession of faith to the pastor.

She did not know what was in store for her, but she soon found out. In many instances, friends and relatives turned against her, and the parents of the children in her school withdrew them. Now she was truly stranded. Her husband had left her unprovided for, because in his last years of failing health he had not been able to earn much money. If the Filicchis had not come to the rescue, things would have gone very hard for her.

There were, however, some Protestant friends who remained loyal to her in New York. Mrs. John Livingston was one; others were Eliza Sadler, Mrs. Startin, and John Wilkes. But the most warm-hearted and generous was Julia Scott. Antonio Filicchi suggested that the family move to Montreal, where he would undertake to pay for the education of Elizabeth's sons, and where he was confident that Elizabeth herself would be able to obtain a teaching position. This plan, however, was changed for a better one; Antonio had talked to Bishop Carroll and Father Dubourg, with the result that Elizabeth could open a school for girls in a house on the grounds of the seminary on Paca Street in Baltimore. As for the boys, Antonio would pay for them at Georgetown, which at that time was a school as well as a college. Though the house on Paca Street as it now stands looks too small—perhaps part of it has been torn down—Elizabeth went there with her three daughters, as well as two of her dead husband's sisters. Cramped though the quarters must have been, a school was started and the situation saved.

Matters turned out even better than that, for Elizabeth had observed at Mass in the seminary chapel (the first Gothic building in America, and considered a gem of architecture) a student who was much older than the others. He was a Samuel Cooper, formerly a sea captain and still a man of some means, who in middle age was soon to be ordained a priest. He also had noticed Mrs. Seton—or "Mother" Seton, as she was already being called, though no religious institute existed—and came forward with an offer to buy for her use as a school a farm at Emmitsburg, about fifty miles west of the city. There would be capacities for expansion, and Elizabeth's two sons could attend Mount St. Mary's, which was only a short distance away.

The idea had already come into being that Elizabeth would form a religious community, one modeled upon the Sisters of Charity, a copy of whose rule had been obtained. But as yet there was, strictly speaking, no habit, the members of the little group merely adopting a garb similar to Mrs. Seton's widows weeds, though as they were so poor, they made them out of any dark cloth that was available. They were still feeling their way, and during this period of development much was makeshift.

At last they set out for Emmitsburg, going towards the hills of western Maryland through Reisterstown, Westminster and Taneytown, until in a valley below them they saw their future home in a valley opposite the "mountain." It was about a mile beyond a cluster of houses known as Emmitsburg. All the women walked, when going up hill, to lighten the load for the horses that drew the prairie schooners—all but Cecelia Seton, as she was in poor health. Elizabeth gave a light-hearted account of the journey in a letter to a friend: "The dear patient was greatly amused with the procession, and all the natives astonished as we went before the carriage. The dogs and the pigs came out to meet us, and the geese stretched their necks in mute demand to know if we were any of their own sort, to which we gave assent."

As the farmhouse that Mr. Cooper had given them was not yet ready for occupancy, Jean Dubois, President of Mount

St. Mary's and later Bishop of New York, gave up his own house to them and moved elsewhere. It was not much of a house—only two roughly plastered rooms—but it served as their residence for six weeks, until they could move into the stone house on their farm. The boys of the school liked to have them there, and Elizabeth Seton and the members of her community continued to go there on fine Sundays for a picnic lunch on some flat rocks halfway up the hill. Then the girls at the school would come, too, and though the boys at Mount St. Mary's were not allowed to mingle with them, this did not prevent some play-acting at "romance." The slaves, who, of course, knew everything, would tell the boys the names of the girls; then the name of an unmet *inamorata* would be scratched on a leaf with a pin.

In the hard winter that often comes to those hills the roads were not only deep with snow, but snow sometimes drifted through the windows of the stone cottage, so that those packed into its rooms awoke to find snow in their rooms when they arose. Food was not plentiful, for, though meat in those days cost only three or four cents a pound at Emmitsburg, even this was too costly for them. The community even had to invent a new kind of "coffee" compounded of molasses and carrot juice. However, they were sometimes able to buy meat from Mr. Dubois—how little is clear from the existing bills—and he would often throw in a chicken. It was he who gave them two turkeys and a goose for their first Christmas dinner.

Cecelia Seton was already a postulant of the community. Their sister Harriet soon became a Catholic, too. She had been engaged to a Dr. Barclay Bayley, Elizabeth Seton's brother. Apparently he was not practicing medicine, but engaged in some sort of mercantile occupation. When he wrote to Cecilia to say that he thought they should wait eight or ten years before they married, so that he could first make his fortune in the West Indies, she realized that this was his way of breaking the engagement. However, her conversion had nothing to do with her disappointment in love.

Like many of the Setons, she came down with tuberculosis, and in anticipation of her death the community was one day wandering about the farm, looking for a suitable spot for her grave. Suddenly, Harriet, who had recently been received into the Church, picked up an apple and threw it at a tree, saying: "Well, there's where *I* want to be buried." And at that very spot her bones now lie. Quite unexpectedly, she was stricken with brain fever and died in a few hours. The shroud already made for Cecelia was used for her instead.

Dubois at first acted as the spiritual director of the Sisters, but when Simon Gabriel Bruté arrived in 1812 for a visit from the seminary at Baltimore, but remained there to teach, Dubois was glad to hand over his work at the convent to the newcomer. Dubois had been a good friend, but he did not have the delicate discernment of Bruté. The forthright American woman and the mercurial Breton became the closest of friends, she alone using the name by which his mother had called him, Gabriel. He would sometimes speak of himself as "poor crazy Bruté," and that was about what many people though him, for, while his vast erudition was much admired at Mount St. Mary's, he was considered as quite unpractical. To Elizabeth he once used the expression, "God's Betty and God's Gabe," at which bit of characteristic quaintness she smiled. But she knew his worth and his profound spirituality; when with her he could to some extent set aside his eccentricity: it was probably only a carapace used as protective armor against conventionally minded people. That he was far from being a mere eccentric he amply proved when he became the first bishop of Vincennes.

In 1810, Cheverus had occasion to go to New York and Philadelphia, and he took that opportunity of visiting Bishop Carroll in Baltimore, from where he came over to Emmitsburg. Mother Seton was told one day that there was a gentleman in the parlor to see her. When she entered the room she knew at once that he was a priest, but did not know that he was a bishop until he told her simply, "I am Cheverus." So this was the man with whom Antonio Filicchi had put her in touch, and who had given her the advice she followed when she became a Catholic five years ago. At once Elizabeth knelt and kissed his hand, overjoyed at having at last met the man who had done so much to resolve her difficulties.

Sorrows were to fall upon Elizabeth Seton in rapid succession. Her eldest daughter Anna Maria had caused her some anxiety by a romance with a young West Indian, who had gone home to Martinique, evidently with no intention of returning. Anina, as she was called, went into a decline and died on March 12, 1812. She was buried in the "Sacred Wood"—to use Bruté's expression, beside Harriet and Cecilia. On her death bed she made her religious vows. Four years later Elizabeth's youngest daughter Rebecca, or Bec, died of a mysterious spinal disease—probably cancer, and cancer of a most painful sort. The child and Father Bruté were very great friends. He happened to be in Baltimore when word of Bec's death was sent by Dubois: "Our angel died this morning a little before four o'clock." Of Elizabeth, Dubois said: "The mother is a miracle of divine favor. Night and day by the child, her health has not appeared to suffer. She held the child in her arms without dropping a tear all the time of her agony and even eight minutes after she had died. *Mulierem fortem.*" To her son William, Elizabeth wrote the month after Bec's death: "It would have been selfish of us to have wished her inexpressible sufferings prolonged and her secure bliss deferred . . . though in her I have lost the little friend of my heart." To Bruté she wrote: "All that the kindest best invention of the most compassionate heart could do has been done by you to carry me through this hard moment which is past and gone as easily as if our high Comforter had spread his soft wings over every fibre." In

October Bec had said, "You know, mother, I never enjoy any little pleasure in this world unless you share it—or I told you of it. How I will beg Him to let me come and comfort you; you know, too, I could guess your pains, even when you did not speak." Later Elizabeth wrote: "She is the liveliest little soul in her worst pains. In the play of her heart she says, 'I consent, dear Lord, to live until You were born,' meaning until Christmas." But God took her before the month was out. When Elizabeth buried her little daughter she said she "could think of nothing but *Te Deum*." She added that her heart was as "still as a calm at sea."

The full fruit of the work Mother Seton initiated was gathered by those who came after her, so that there are now at least eight distinct branches of the Sisters of Charity, conducting schools, colleges, orphanages and hospitals. One thing needs to be specially noted: for the children at Emmitsburg Elizabeth opened a free school, which may be said to have been the first American parochial school. While it is true that there were previously one or two schools connected with Catholic parishes, they normally made some small charge; the parochial school at Emmitsburg made none whatever. And when St. Joseph's came to have a high school (it is strictly a college now) any local girl who had reached that level of education paid nothing.

Elizabeth gave a scholarship at Mount St. Mary's to a boy from New York whose mother was a widow, and paid for his clothing as well. She also took a keen interest in young Jerome Bonaparte, a nephew of Emperor Napoleon. We have his undated letter to her asking for an *Agnus Dei;* he promised to keep it "as a memorial of kindness and love for your little child who always thinks of you with respect and love and will think of you with gratitude also, especially if I shall have an Agnus Dei from you as a present." On the back of this letter Elizabeth wrote: "Dear Jerome, I earnestly beg our Lord to preserve you in the graces He has so tenderly bestowed upon you—take care not to lose them. Pray for me and I will pray for you. Yr. true friend E A S."

Elizabeth's own sons, after finishing at Mount St. Mary's, were given employment by Antonio Filicchi, Richard in his counting house, and William—because of his more adventurous disposition—in one of Antonio's trading vessels. About William his mother was at times anxious, though she used to say that she would have liked to have traveled like St. Francis Xavier. In a letter written in the last year of her life she exclaimed: "William, William, William . . . To lose you here for a few years of so embittered life is but the common lot, but to love as I love you and to lose you forever—oh, unutterable anguish! . . . My William, William, William, if I did not see your doting Bec and Nina above what would save my heart from breaking?" This son was to become the father of the Archbishop Seton who died in 1927 when he was nearing ninety.

Elizabeth's own health was now precarious, but since 1818 she had lived in such a state of resignation as greatly to gain spiritually. It was not until the late summer of 1820 that her last illness began. A school building for the day students was going up, and Dubois urged her to climb upon a pile of lumber so as to get a good view of what the carpenters were doing. It was an unseasonably cold day, and when the wind struck her she felt touched by death. In September, Bruté heard her general confession (the previous month Dubois had given her extreme unction).

Yet she lingered on, at times feeling well enough to write letters of farewell to close friends—among them Cheverus, Dubourg (now a bishop in the West), Flaget, and Filicchi. She welcomed, as always, the New Year with great hope, but her condition did not improve, so that Dubois anointed her again on January 2. The following day Bruté began a retreat for the children who were to make their first Communion on the Feast of the Epiphany, and knowing how much she loved that day, he encouraged her to believe that she would live to receive Communion herself that day. It was not to be; during the night she began to sink rapidly, and in the small hours of the morning she died peacefully without any struggle. It was January 4, 1821; she was only forty-six.

Baltimore

J. Carroll A
Leonard Neale A
A. Maréchal F

Boston Cheverus F
Philadelphia Egan I
New York
Bardstown Flaget F
Cincinnati Fenwick
St. Louis Rosati Ita
Richmond Pat Kelly I
Charleston England I

IX: John England

(1786–1842)

John Carroll, when his enormous diocese was subdivided in 1808, was obliged to recommend, as the men most suitable to head the new dioceses, men who were—with one exception—Frenchmen. And his recommendations were excellent: Cheverus for Boston, Flaget for Bardstown. But a Franciscan, Michael Egan, an Irishman, was recommended for Philadelphia, and the Congregation of Propaganda chose two Irish Dominicans in succession for New York. And when Carroll died, his coadjutor, Leonard Neale, a Marylander like himself, succeeded him as Archbishop of Baltimore. When Neale died two years later, the Baltimore Sulpician, Ambrose Marechal, took his place. With that the French domination of the Catholic Church in America may be said to have begun, though since Fenwick was chosen for Cincinnati and the Italian, Rosati, for St. Louis, it is clear that there was no thought of a French hegemony for the Church in America.

Such a plan was, however, suspected, and greatly resented by many of the Irish in the East; suspicions were increased by the somewhat stiff and uncompromising character of Archbishop Marechal, and his alleged contempt for the Irish. While the resentment of the Irish was by no means universal, it came to a head when Virginia and the Carolinas seemed veering toward the danger of schism. Virginia need not concern us, as the bishop sent out to the newly created see of Richmond, Patrick Kelly, gave up after little more than a year, feeling himself unable to cope with his difficulties.

The administration of his diocese then reverted to Marechal. It was quite different in the case of Charleston, South Carolina. The man sent there as bishop, John England, found means of averting the threatened schism, though by means that did not commend themselves to his metropolitan.

An element of play-acting may have been involved; the priests and people of Charleston (who were to some extent backed by those in Virginia) may have used the threat of schism as a means of scaring Rome. Yet the malcontents may have felt that they had gone too far to back down, had it not been for the action of Propaganda. At all events, the threat was taken quite seriously, as it involved the setting up of an independent Catholic Church. The Holy See acted promptly, especially as Archbishop Marechal was clearly not a man ever likely to throw oil on troubled waters. John England, because of his tact and versatile ability and immense energy, proved to be just the man capable of dealing with the situation.

Trusteeism was, of course, a large part of the trouble. But the main factor in the case was that the French priest at Norfolk, Virginia, James Lucas, and another French priest, Joseph Picot de Clorivière, at Charleston, were unpopular, chiefly, it would seem, because they were Frenchmen and protégés of the Archbishop of Baltimore. To all pleas that they be withdrawn Marechal turned a deaf ear, all the more deaf because this was another instance of the trustees demanding the right to choose their own pastors.

No serious trouble would have occurred had not newcomers to the United States got it into their heads that the methods of American democracy extended even to ecclesiastical matters. While the Church here, far from objecting to democracy, thrives under it, one must indicate the fact that the government of the Church itself is necessarily hierarchical —a point which the muddled and violent heads at Charleston did not grasp.

The two Irish priests at Charleston were very able men, whatever their other faults may have been. From them emanated the idea of an apostolic delegation to the United States and the founding of a Catholic University at Washington—both excellent ideas, though the time for them was not yet ripe.

But a fantastic project eventuated: an Irish Dominican in New York named Thomas Carbry was sent a suggestion that he go to Holland, and make plans for the eventual—though as soon as possible—establishment of an independent Catholic Church. A further letter was sent to the Holy See, which said that the reason Carbry should be made a bishop was that "he has, with us, the peculiar merit of being obnoxious to the Baltimore junta." The ingenious plot (if it was really seriously intended) completely misfired. Carbry sent on the letter he had received from Charleston to a friend in Ireland, and that friend forwarded it to Rome. The authorities there were deeply disturbed, and, as it was evident that there was intense antagonism to Marechal, two Irishmen were consecrated, one for Richmond, and the other for Charleston.

John England had already distinguished himself in Cork as a preacher, as the editor of a Catholic monthly, and as a professor in the diocesan seminary. With his arrival at the end of 1820 the project of the independent Catholic Church of America immediately dissolved. Charleston was not long in finding out what kind of a man John England was.

He was completely unstereotyped and therefore very different from the rigidly correct Marechal, who did not altogether approve of him, or rather, of his methods. For instance, Marechal did not at all like England's drawing up a constitution for his diocese, though this proved to be eminently wise, the situation being what it was at that time. Taking the convocation of the Church of England as his model—though, obviously, with some modifications—he set up a house of laymen and another of the clergy. By this means those who thirsted for distinction were made to feel important, and were free to orate to their hearts' content, while the final decision on matters was left to the bishop. In short, theirs was merely a consultative and not a definitive power, as is true of any diocesan council. John England was glad to know the opinion of these assemblies, but, while willing to be guided by it when it seemed to him to be well founded, was not bound by it.

Bishop England also started the first Catholic magazine in the United States, for Père Richard's little newspaper at Detroit was quite short-lived. In this he was ably assisted by his sister Joanna, who sank her small fortune in the venture and was quite capable of conducting the magazine during her brother's frequent absences. Though the journal, by modern standards, left much to be desired, it became very influential.

Then, not satisfied with the French methods of training in the seminary at Baltimore, he founded a seminary of his own. Young Americans who offered themselves were heartily welcome, as were seminarians who came from Ireland, but he wished all to receive their training under his direct supervision. As suitable professors were not easy to find, he had to do much of the teaching himself, though this involved "boning up" on subjects that he had forgotten, sometimes by reading textbooks only a day in advance of the matter to be treated in the classroom. That this method had defects is not to be denied, but there was an advantage that was a great compensation: the bishop came into close and affectionate personal contact with the future priests of his diocese and could assure himself of their devoted service.

Trusteeism was still a serious problem, found everywhere, though it was not too hampering when the right sort of trustees were found. His diocesan constitution served to remove many of its evils in the Charleston area, but it was apparent to him that a provincial council should be summoned, so that the American hierarchy might adopt a uniform policy. To this the Archbishop of Baltimore could not be brought to agree. He thought of England as an officious young Irishman and, because of what he had had to suffer, he was by now disgruntled with Irish priests. Not until Marechal died, and the Englishman James Whitfield succeeded him to the see of Baltimore in 1828, was it possible to summon the First Provincial Council of Baltimore, and thus to clear the air.

John England had arrived from Ireland with a considerable reputation; what he accomplished at Charleston augmented the esteem in which he was held. Indeed, it began to be thought that he was much too able a man to be left buried in the South, and when Connolly died in 1825, it was hoped that England would succeed him in New York. England himself entertained this hope, partly because he perceived that in a more populous centre his opportunities for fruitful work would be much greater, but also because the climate of South Carolina did not agree with him. It meant little or nothing to him that at Charleston his salary as bishop was only $1,000 a year, but he was constantly embarrassed by lack of funds to carry out his undertakings. His necessities were partly relieved when Pope Leo XII sent him 500 crowns; even so, he could meet his obligations only by imposing a tax of fifty cents a quarter on every man in the diocese. As may be realized, that did not bring in a great deal, yet upon it the seminary was mainly supported. By 1829 he was saddled with a debt of $6,500.

Nevertheless, the diocese had grown. His report of 1829 showed that the three priests of the diocese had increased to ten. He had sixteen churches already existing or in preparation, where previously there had been only four; the number of communicants had mounted from 375 in 1820 to 1150. The growth could scarcely be described as spectacular, but England had the satisfaction of having made 200 converts and of knowing that the diocese which he himself described as "the largest and the poorest in the Union" had now been brought into fairly good order.

He had been careful not to take sides in the antagonism that still sometimes existed between the Irish and the French, but his private opinion was that the French and the American spirit were irreconcilable, and that—largely on this account—in the eyes of most non-Catholics the Catholic Church seemed foreign and exotic. He believed, despite the unruliness of certain unfortunate exceptions, that it was the Irish newcomers who were most readily assimilated as Americans. One of the main difficulties, he thought, was the lack of educational facilities. Though the Jesuits had colleges in Washington and in St. Louis, and the Dominicans one in Kentucky, while there were other colleges or seminaries at Emmitsburg and Bardstown, most of these were too far away to be of much use to him. He struggled manfully against his difficulties, but could not help sometimes feeling depressed.

Though he sometimes, understandably, gave vent to angry feeling and deep gloom—that progress was too slow, he was able to move things forward. Soon he began to make himself felt throughout the whole country. In fact he was, without setting himself up in that role, the man who, perhaps more than any other, marked the beginning of a new era in American Catholic history. For one thing, the domination of French bishops, since the appearance of Marechal in 1817, was drawing to a close. And though it would be most ungrateful to forget Cheverus at Boston, or Flaget and Dubourg and David in the West (and they were soon to be joined by Bruté), and the French bishops who in a later period achieved great things in the United States, ecclesiastical control was about to pass into the hands of Irishmen. Though it was mainly against them that the Nativist fury was to be directed, with racial antagonism subsequently occurring between the Irish and the Germans of the Middle West, nevertheless the

Irish, the largest of the immigrant groups, became the chief leavening factor in the Catholic Church in America.

In North Carolina sparsely settled by Catholics, there was in New Berne, in the person of William Gaston, a distinguished layman whose influence extended far beyond the confines of his own state. His father was a doctor of Huguenot origin, who had come to this country before the Revolution, long enough to be thoroughly American in feeling. He had married an English wife who had been educated in France and was staunchly Catholic, and who had brought her children up to be as devout as herself.

When Georgetown was opened in 1791 young William Gaston was enrolled as its first student. At Carroll's advice he went to Princeton, where he graduated, and in 1825 received an honorary degree from Harvard. So eminent was he that in 1828 he was spoken of as a possible Ambassador to the Court of St. James, and might actually have been appointed had it not been, as one of his friends put it, that North Carolina was "so buried . . . in the slough of Jacksonism that the administration will be cautious." However, a little later he did become Chief Justice of the state Supreme Court. An attempt was made to prevent this by using the North Carolina Constitution of 1776 against him—this stipulated that officeholders must subscribe to "the truths of the Protestant religion." The attempt to disqualify him because of his religion failed miserably. But, for that matter, the Catholic Dr. Thomas Burke had earlier represented North Carolina in the Continental Congress and in 1781 was elected governor, while his cousin Aedanus Burke, another Catholic, became Chief Justice of the state.

Gaston was considered as Chief Justice Marshall's successor, but another Catholic, Roger B. Taney, obtained the high office. Marshall had expressed a willingness to retire if he was sure that the North Carolinian would take his place.

The fact of the matter was that Gaston was known to prefer to serve his own state. It was for this reason that he declined to go to Washington as senator in 1840. This reason also operated when Henry Clay was about to run for the presidency, and was ready to take Gaston as his running mate, though a stronger reason probably was that he feared the Whigs would lose if burdened with a Catholic; as it was, Polk was elected president, with a margin of little more than one per cent of the popular vote. Gaston did not live long after that, and England died in 1842, but through all the twenty-two years he occupied the see of Charleston, Gaston was a close friend and a tower of strength.

It was not, of course, merely because Gaston spoke of him so highly to his friends in Washington that John England attained his national reputation. The other facts that have been mentioned here all contributed—perhaps most of all his fame as on orator. He was able to top off a speech of lucid cogency with the "spread eagle" peroration which the America of his day much admired. Among the great speeches he made was one to the House of Representatives on January 8, 1826, President John Quincy Adams coming to hear him. England spoke, not on some innocuous topic, but on the Catholic Church.

Though a turbulent antagonism to Catholicism had begun to arise, this was more prevalent in the cities of the North than anywhere else, and even there had not yet mounted to its height. The better read Americans—among whom were Calhoun and Webster and Clay—knew of the esteem in which Catholics had been held during the early days of the republic; besides, they had minds too noble to be infected with religious prejudice. This good will was further shown by the appointment of Charles Constantine Pise to be chaplain of the United States Senate, the only Catholic ever to hold this position. That he had written a five-volume history of the Catholic Church, largely from notes put at his disposal by

Simon Bruté, may have helped. Only three years later, however, the fact that General Harrison paid a visit to Mount St. Mary's resulted in a strongly-worded petition of protest being presented to Congress, against an action which was totally without religious significance.

John England, though he was not much bothered in the South with anti-Catholic outbursts, suffered criticism rather from a few of his brother bishops. We have seen how set Archbishop Marechal was against calling a provincial council, and though his successor, Whitfield, summoned two, in 1829 and again in 1833, the spirit observable in the second led Bishop Kenrick of Philadelphia to write early in 1834 to Cardinal Cullen in Ireland. He said: "The talents, learning, fame, eloquence of Bp. England rendered him not an object of envy, for I believe the good prelates superior to this narrow passion, but fear, for they dreaded lest his active mind and liberal views might lead them into the adoption of measures that might weaken their authority and disturb the repose of the Church." Kenrick so heartily admired England that he told Cullen, "I would at any moment resign my mitre to make place for him."

X: Prince Gallitzin, alias Mr. Smith

(1770–1840)

Stephen Theodore Badin enjoys the distinction of being the first man to be ordained a priest in the United States, where he arrived as a deacon; Prince Gallitzin was the first to receive all the orders here. Both men went to the frontier—Badin to the more distant but more thickly settled frontier of Kentucky; Gallitzin to the much nearer but even more rugged frontier on the Alleghenies. Each was offered a bishopric but declined.

Gallitzin is not being written about here because he was a Russian prince, nor because he sank a considerable fortune in his mountain parish, but because he was an extraordinary personality, if not the exalted personage he would inevitably have become had he yielded to the pleading of his family and returned to Europe. Even there he would undoubtedly have been unable to repress all his quirks of character, but the wild and woolly America of the early nineteenth century exactly suited him.

Gallitzin did not go to the frontier at once, but worked for brief periods at Port Tobacco and Taneytown (both in Maryland) and Connewago, Pennsylvania, clearly restless until he was able to find what was to his liking, the Catholic settlement he established among the mountains. One suspects that this was partly because as an aristocrat (of a somewhat dictatorial sort on occasion) he wanted to have a completely free hand, and that he did not act as he did because of a sociological theory, of which he probably never heard. The name "Mr. Smith," which he assumed, points to humility, or at least to his seeing that his princedom might hamper his work as a priest. And we hear of such ascetic practices as wearing a hairshirt and usually sleeping on the floor, though he kept these secret as long as he could and, when discovered, passed them off lightly.

We should know little about him were it not for his first biographer Peter Henry Lemcke, who joined him as his assistant in 1834. Lemcke was good-humored and good-natured enough to be able to get along very well with this "queer old saint" as Bishop Kenrick called him; indeed, he seems to have been something of a connoisseur of eccentricity. He tells of the old man's rash and harsh mannerisms and his flaming eyes, but he also saw that Gallitzin had the gift of tears and that this seemed to increase as he neared his end.

In truth, Prince Gallitzin was full of seeming contradictions: though a man of boundless charity, he was a good deal of a martinet in the way he ruled his small world. He insisted that his people address him as Mr. Smith, yet, if anybody forgot that he was really Prince Gallitzin, he soon found out that Mr. Smith had not forgotten that fact. He was inclined to be short-tempered; then his deeply sunken eyes would flash and the old lion would roar; but it was all over in a moment. In the parish there lived several pious old ladies who had no occupation except that of looking after the prince's few and very simple wants. Their main duty was to keep away the hordes of vagabonds who otherwise would have stripped him of everything; but they could not prevent him taking the shirt off his back for a beggar who had managed to get through the cordon. Though he was grateful for their devotion, they were not spared his abuse, especially if he thought they had exceeded their authority. However, they did not seem to mind, though they gave their services without pay.

It was largely because of them that he died solvent. He was a man who would have given everything away if he had been unchecked. He was never a good financial manager, and often disposed of plots on his large tract of land for next to nothing or at prices much below what he should have charged. He had gone heavily into debt in confident expectation that he eventually would be a rich man, but, as his father had died intestate, he was deprived of his patrimony under Russian law, since he was a Catholic priest. Gallitzin's mother sent him money from time to time, as did his sister up to the time of her marriage. Gallitzin's debts weighed heavily on him for many years, and he saw no way of ever becoming able to meet them. However, the King of the Netherlands, a boyhood friend, came to his rescue, along with Henry Clay and the Russian ambassador to Washington, Baron von Tuyl.

His earlier life in Russia had not been very happy for Demetrius Augustine Gallitzin. His father was one of the more illustrious of the Russian aristocracy and served as Catherine the Great's ambassador to The Hague. His mother, daughter of a Prussian field marshal, was a convert, who tried actively to bring all her friends—including D'Alembert and Goethe—into the Church. She had more success with her son, who also became a Catholic. The family's home life was not too close, however, and perhaps because of this the young prince was successful in persuading his parents to let him make a grand tour in the United States, accompanied by a priest. The young prince got no farther than Baltimore, where he entered the seminary, apparently on a sudden impulse, though he was well aware that this cut him off from any career in the Russian army or diplomatic service.

His priesthood was not at all of the kind that the Sulpicians at Baltimore, or its archbishop, envisioned. He could have gone back to Europe—and was pressed by his father to do so—as there his rank would have assured him rapid promotion. Perhaps it was to make things easy for the aristocrat, accustomed to a comfortable life, that his first appointments were to quiet places in the East, where he could have at least some of the amenities of civilization, instead of the frontier, with its great hardships. Yet, as he showed himself dissatisfied, he was allowed to go off to the wilds of the Alleghenies to establish a colony on a large tract of land. There the hitherto restless man remained for the rest of his life.

America was full of settlements of one kind and another—some of them hair-brained schemes which did not last long. At least one of these was started under Catholic auspices, at Gallipolis on the Ohio river, though that, too, failed miserably in the end. Gallitzin had little ready money available, but, confident of having a good deal eventually, his credit was excellent. He was able to buy land cheap, and sell it without profit, or at a loss, to the people who flocked to him. For their benefit, he set up a woodyard, a tannery and a flour mill at his own expense. His project soon was a success, as word about it got around, whatever its financial defects.

In all this there was, it is hardly necessary to say, perfect good faith. Gallitzin borrowed freely because he was sure that his wealthy father would cover all his obligations, and his creditors were fully assured that this was the case. The plans themselves were perfectly feasible; and the burning-eyed young priest who spoke so persuasively with an air of authority was not to be thought of as a mere visionary. When he first found himself deeply in debt this did not trouble him unduly, for he would clear everything up when his father died and he obtained his share of the inheritance. So confident was he about this that at a time when he owed $2000 he was able to make a donation of $200 towards the building of a seminary in Philadelphia. But when his father died the following year, he discovered that, as no will had been left, under the complexities of Russian law he was to get nothing from the estate.

That difficulty possibly could have been surmounted had he been able to go in person to Russia, where his father had many influential friends. But this was the one thing he dared not do: had he gone there to plead his own cause, he would certainly have been arrested as a deserter, for when years earlier he had received official notice to join the regiment in which he held Catherine the Great's commission as an officer, he had ignored it.

Though the prince in his youth had never performed any military service, his father had at least seen to it that he was taught the use of foil and sabre by competent instructors. He had learned enough to drill a company of men at his mountain settlement and to teach them the use of a sabre when they were gettting ready to join the American army during the war of 1812.

Yet though most of his people admired him wholeheartedly, there were one or two unmannerly fellows during the early years of the settlement who threatened him with violence, presumably when they were in their cups. And his whims now and then made it hard for people to get along with him. He was inclined to be rather touchy. He once took offense with Bishop Kenrick, who had appointed him his vicar-general for the mountains. He did so when the bishop, merely out of consideration, sent him an assistant, his intention being that of sparing a failing old man from being obliged to make long journeys from his headquarters. But Gallitzin misunderstood what was in Kenrick's mind, and when he thought he had discovered an intrigue on the part of an inn-keeper with whom the assistant priest was lodging, he wrote to the Bishop in his most icy style: "Since it has pleased his Lordship to make a tavern-keeper vicar-general of the mountains, and there was no need of two, he begged to resign his position as vicar-general."

A young German priest who had been sent recognized the prince's eccentricities, and they soon hit it off perfectly together. This is clear even in the account that Peter Lemcke left of the first meeting between them, and during all the years that they spent together, so far from there being any occasion for Lemcke's taking offense, he enjoyed the society of Gallitzin as much as he venerated him.

In his account of their first meeting he tells how, when coming on a September morning towards Loretto, he saw approaching in a horse-drawn sled over the rough road a shabby old man, whose very hat, he said, a beggar would have disdained to pick from the gutter; this, he was told, was the priest he was looking for. Riding up to him, Lemcke asked: "Are you really the pastor of Loretto?"

When the shabby old man told him that he was, Lemcke asked again: "Prince Gallitzin?"

The venerable priest laughed and answered: "I am that very exalted personage."

Then Gallitzin explained that he had to get around like that because he could not use a carriage on the rocky mountain roads, and that he had not been able to mount a horse since a fall. What he did not explain just then was that after the fall he had had a bad hernia. He was obliged to use the sled because he had to carry in it everything he required for saying Mass.

Lemcke accompanied him to his Mass at a small private house. Before it began, those who had assembled made their confession in the large kitchen where baking and cooking were simultaneously going on. Those waiting to make their confession knelt in the woodshed or under the trees, their prayer books in their hands. This was Lemcke's first sight of mission work on that frontier, and he was astonished as well as edified. After Mass, Prince Gallitzin preached, and then baptized several children. Finally, a dinner table was set up where the portable altar had been, and the congregation was served dinner in relays—into well late in the day.

To Lemcke the scene was enchanting in its fervor and simplicity, reminding him of the love-feasts of the Church in primitive times. It was night when he got back with Gallitzin to Loretto. The prince invited his visitor to stay with him that night, and later Lemcke discovered what an unusual honor this was, for it was one of Gallitzin's eccentricities to prefer to have the house to himself, despite his invalidism. The two men sat up late, charmed with one another, and as it was forty-two years since Gallitzin had last been in Europe they found a good deal to talk about. In the morning the prince came to his guest's room, carrying an armful of wood. And when Lemcke entered the little chapel to say Mass, the prince insisted on acting as his server.

One of the surprising things that Lemcke tells us is that the prince's parents considered him to have been rather "empty." However, "empty" does not seem to be the right word, unless it means that the lad went mooning about the place, at loose ends, apparently without an object in life. He had no thought of the priesthood until he met Bishop Carroll; then his seminary training and his work as a priest—especially that in the mountains—revealed unsuspected depths in his character. As he told Lemcke, he became a "changed man"—changed in a way that surprised even himself.

The polemical writing that Gallitzin did in English is hardly worth examining in detail, yet one can see that it was effective at the time and that he managed to express himself with pungency and pith. English was the only language that he knew well, except for Latin. He had forgotten the "high German" he had spoken in his boyhood, and at Loretto he heard mostly the "Pennsylvania Dutch" which Lemcke found distressing. Russian he did not know at all, for his father, like all Russians of the upper classes, generally used French, and that, too, he had mostly forgotten, if he had ever known much of it. But his sermons in English, though he was no orator, were forceful and to the point.

He ignored his ill health, continuing to bump along in his sled on the rough mountain roads. As he disregarded the precautions he should have taken, and did not submit in time to an operation, it was from strangulated hernia that he died.

Lemcke was with Gallitzin at the end, and tells of weeping people coming in one by one to get his blessing. To one man he would give no blessing; instead he silently shook his finger at him. The rebuke cured him of the habitual drunkenness that Gallitzin had so often reproved. This time the man fell to his knees, promising amendment. Lemcke, bending over the dying man, heard him whisper, "Poor fellow: I did not remember him in my will. See that he is not forgotten—if something can be done."

Lemcke stayed that night with his friend. At midnight he said Mass in Prince Gallitzin's room and gave him Holy Communion. The dying man still lingered on, and still a procession of weeping people came for his blessing. After the Prayers for a Departing Soul, Demetrius Augustine Gallitzin gave back his soul to his Maker. Lemcke, kneeling beside him with a lighted candle in his hand, felt the flickering pulse fail; Prince Gallitzin had passed away without a sign of struggle. It was May 6, 1840.

XI: John Hughes

(1797–1864)

John Hughes was born in a village in County Tyrone on June 24, 1797, and even as a small boy had the ambition of becoming a priest, for which purpose he was eager to obtain all the education he could. However, it was not until he was on towards manhood that he had any very clear idea how his ambition might be attained; this was after the emigration of his family to Chambersburg, Pennsylvania, about ten miles north of the Maryland border. While there, he heard of Mount St. Mary's at Emmitsburg, only twenty miles or so to the southeast. It was the kind of institution he was looking for.

Though it styled itself a college, and conferred degrees on older students, it also accepted quite small boys, and also trained young men for the priesthood. As some of the seminarians paid their way by teaching the schoolboys, this seemed to make it a likely place for the son of a peddler. The rawboned peasant lad was refused upon his first application, but at the same time told that there might be a vacancy later. He took lodgings in Emmitsburg, so as to be at hand should such a vacancy occur, meanwhile working on a small bridge on the Taneytown road.

Jean Dubois, President of Mount St. Mary's, was one of a number of French priests who had sought refuge in this country during the disturbances in his own. Arriving with a letter of introduction from Lafayette, he was accepted by the general's friends—the Lees and Randolphs of Virginia among them, through their influence being even permitted to say

Mass in the capitol at Richmond. He received lessons in English from no less a person than Patrick Henry, giving lessons in French in return.

He then transferred to Maryland, where Catholics were far more numerous. After working for a while in Frederick, he was able to buy a hillside near the village of Emmitsburg, and there he opened a school and college, at first in a very small way. But as the students increased in numbers, he tried to persuade the Sulpicians at Baltimore to accept it as their minor seminary, for in 1808 he had joined the Sulpicians himself. As this would have meant that they would have had to accept financial responsibility, the Sulpicians declined, so Mount St. Mary's, being independent, was free to give the courses necessary for the priesthood. Dubois and his associates regretfully severed their connection with the Society, though remaining on the best of terms with the priests at the Baltimore seminary.

The second time that Hughes applied to Dubois, it was decided that he was not yet sufficiently advanced in his studies, but he was offered a job as overseer of slaves. He could live in a one-room shack overlooking the vegetable garden where the slaves worked and was promised the loan of books. As this was a step nearer to what he wanted, Hughes was glad to accept. He knew more about gardening, having been brought up on a farm in Ireland, than about building bridges.

His duties as overseer were not onerous. From the window of his shack he always had the slaves in view—and though only two of them, Timothy and Peter, actually belonged to Dubois, several fathers who had sons there as students paid their bills by lending slaves to the institution. Hughes did not have much more to do than look up from his book now and then, and so made rapid progress. Dubois, happening to drop in one day, was surprised to discover how well the assiduous Hughes had done, and decided that this raw-boned youth would be of more use as a seminarian and a teacher of the boys than as a supervisor of slaves. This was about 1820.

As a student, Hughes' application enabled him to outstrip more showily brilliant men, and when he reached theology he had the advantage of having as his professor Simon Bruté, a man whose range of knowledge, enthusiasm and sensitive insight were probably not equaled at that time in America. Moreover, though Hughes was not very popular with many of the students and some of the professors, perhaps because he was Irish he was better able to hit it off with a Breton than with anybody else. So long as Bruté lived Hughes was always able to rely upon him for correction and advice.

Yet in many ways the two Celts were very dissimilar. Where Hughes was always hard-headed and practical, Bruté was regarded as an irresponsible eccentric. Bruté did not much like the way that Hughes was so easily drawn, even while at Mount St. Mary's, into acrimonious controversy. Recognizing his pupil's zeal, however, Bruté never refused his assistance.

Hughes showed not only belligerence, but courage. During a fire at the Mount he ventured so near the flames that he burned a hole in his coat. As he possessed only one suit, he wore this with a patch. This did not matter much at a place where everybody, except a few well-to-do students, was rather shabby.

After ordination to the priesthood, Hughes was appointed to a church in Philadelphia, and that was a centre where the young priest had ample opportunities of showing what was in him. In fact, Bishop Conwell, when in Rome in 1829, suggested that Hughes be appointed his coadjutor. The suggestion was not accepted, Francis Patrick Kenrick being chosen instead. Kenrick was not only made coadjutor but Conwell, because of his weak handling of the Hogan schism, was deprived of all episcopal authority though he remained nominally Bishop of Philadelphia.

John Hughes took no direct part in the trusteeism issue

that had caused all the turmoil. However, under Kenrick, he built a new church (St. John's) in which he took good care to see that there was no board of lay trustees. That pointed the way to the destruction of the obnoxious system; what was less fortunate was that, when he departed from Philadelphia in 1837, St. John's was under a crushing load of debt. However, Hughes impressed everybody by his energy and ability, especially as a controversialist. It was clear that he was marked out for great achievements.

The friendly feeling that had existed between Catholics and Protestants during the Revolution and the early years of the republic had considerably altered, largely due to the arrival of many Catholic emigrants who had in many cases come to the United States, feeling that the Constitution guaranteed religious freedom to all. In spite of this, the mood of people in the large cities, where most of the new arrivals, especially the Irish, were settling, was becoming rather ugly. Though no violence had as yet occurred, the vituperation of bigots warned that outbursts might be expected, fomented by the constant vilification of all things Catholic. Hughes lost no time in striking powerful blows for his religion, and was soon swept — not altogether unwillingly — into the war of pamphleteering and platform debate. For example, he stood up to the famous Presbyterian controversialist, Robert J. Breckinridge, first in a duel in the newspapers and then in a lecture hall. This was an error of judgment, for Breckinridge did not hesitate to bring the foulest charges against Catholics, with the result that Hughes, never a very placable man, lost his temper and descended to personalities. The wise and mild Bruté had warned him against this, but Hughes felt impelled to act as he did, thereby merely stirring up further animosity.

He also played a hoax in 1830 when he sent to a virulent sheet called *The Protestant* a series of articles under the pseudonym of "Cranmer." In these articles, while making an ostensible attack upon the Church, he carefully introduced absurdities which the editor should have recognized as such, but instead gobbled down greedily. Only when he had grown tired of the performance did Hughes announce that he had perpetuated a hoax, and that the way this had been taken proved how gullible were the enemies of the Church. *The Protestant* tried to bluster the matter through by saying that Hughes was not "Cranmer," or if he was, it only showed how adept he was in "Jesuitical" deceit. He also published an anonymous novel —mere propaganda, and of a kind hardly worth reading now, but which may have served its purpose at the time.

Jean Dubois, the former President of Mount St. Mary's, was appointed to New York, and it was at his request that Hughes was sent as his coadjutor in 1837—not a whit too soon, as Dubois was in his seventies and in failing health. But when a directive came from Rome that the coadjutor was to decide all administrative questions, as Dubois was paralyzed following a stroke, the titular bishop was stricken to the heart by his humiliation. Hughes had been very impressive in the eyes of Dubois, when he regarded him at a distance, but things were different when he had the energetic Hughes living in the same house with him on Mott Street. There were constant irritants, and Dubois probably brought himself to believe that if he had been pushed into the background it was through intrigue on the part of Hughes. Naturally, this seemed a treacherous betrayal on the part of his protégé.

Dubois had not shone as an executive, even at Mount St. Mary's, though he must have been better in this respect than was commonly supposed, to have built up the place so well. But it was one thing to deal with young students, to whom his word was law and when he was in the prime of his life, and something vastly different to control unruly trustees. It was even a question, when he arrived as bishop in New York, whether all the churches would admit him. He was a Frenchman and the 35,000 Catholics in the city, who were overwhelmingly Irish, would have much preferred their brilliant fellow countryman, Father Power, who had acted as administrator of the diocese during the interregnum between Connolly's death in February, 1826, and the consecration of Dubois in October. Moreover, after all his years in the United States, his pronounciation of English was far from perfect.

It was no easy matter to manage the affairs of a diocese that comprised two states—New York and New Jersey—and in which there were 150,000 Catholics, served by nine churches, only three of which were in New York City itself. Yet Dubois manfully grappled with his problems, and as every ship brought many new immigrants and very few priests, the bishop decided to found his own seminary, an activity about which he already knew a good deal. In this he was very unlucky: the house he was remodeling at Nyack burned to the ground before it was ready for occupancy. With it went up in smoke the $18,000 contributed to the project by the Society of the Propagation of the Faith. After that there was a wild idea of starting again on a site near the Thousand Islands. Not until John Hughes arrived and bought Rose Hill Farm at Fordham (the nucleus of the present university) was a real start made. Even that, however, was not a success as a seminary, and was sold to the Jesuits of Kentucky, and a former Methodist institution at Troy bought for a song. Not until, much later, Archbishop Corrigan built Dunwoodie was New York's seminary problem satisfactorily solved.

Dubois had quickly run headlong into trusteeism. Indeed, when he suspended a refractory priest named Levins, pastor of the Cathedral parish, in 1834 the trustees threatened to withhold the bishop's salary. To this Dubois made the grand answer: "Well, gentlemen, you may vote my salary or not, just as seems good to you. I am an old man and do not need much. I can live in a basement or a garret. But whether I come up from the basement or down from the garret, I shall still be your bishop." In that particular issue the old man won, but it took the firm hand of Hughes finally to bridle the trustees.

Dubois was very angry at being superannuated, and though in the end he submitted, it was, as he put it, "taking the bit but not until he had covered it with blood." Yet it was most fortunate that, during the tumultuous days that were beginning, New York's guidance was in the hands of so able and courageous a bishop as John Hughes. The violent storm of Nativism was beginning. On August 11, 1834, the Ursuline convent at Charlestown, Massachusetts, was burned to the ground, the firemen doing nothing to help the Sisters or their pupils, many of whom belonged to the most select Unitarian families of Boston. The crime not only went unpunished, but, when one of the ringleaders of the mob was found not guilty at his trial, there were cheers in court, and the criminal was showered with so many presents by sympathizers that he was obliged to thank them with a notice in the papers.

Still worse occurred in Philadelphia when a mob protested against Bishop Kenrick's objection to Catholic children in the public schools being obliged to listen to the reading of the King James version of the Bible. This was interpreted as a Catholic attack on the Bible itself. Some opponents roared that this was the signal for a new St. Bartholomew's Day massacre. So, by way of protecting themselves against such horrors, the mob rioted for several days, burning a number of churches and convents, and whole rows of houses in the sections occupied by the Irish, before order was restored by the militia.

Bishop Hughes, who by this time had succeeded Dubois as Bishop of New York, blamed the mildness of Kenrick for much that had happened. He was sometimes called "dagger John" because, like all bishops, he signed his name with a cross, and he rose to the occasion in characteristic fashion. He posted a thousand armed men around every Catholic church, and then told the mayor what he had done.

"Are you afraid?" sneered Mayor Harper. "Yes," the bishop replied. "Not for my churches, but for yours. If a single Catholic church is burned here, New York will be turned into another Moscow." That ended the matter, except for a few fist-fights between individual Catholics and Protestants.

Much of the uproar was due to the publication of a number of anti-Catholic books of so vile a character that they are no longer to be found except in bookstores that specialize in pornography. Of these the most infamous was the *Awful Disclosures* of Maria Monk, published in 1836, who alleged that she had been a nun at a convent in Montreal known as the Hotel Dieu. After a short time, the imposter was completely discredited.

Nevertheless, the Nativist movement continued to grow. The argument was that the United States was being swamped with immigrants—most of them Catholics—who competed on unfair terms with American-born workmen. A political party was formed, popularly known as the Know-Nothings, which had considerable success in several states and had even nominated a presidential candidate. The outbreak of the Civil War ended its brief political success. But in 1854, its peak year, it elected in Massachusetts the governor, the entire senate and most of the members of the lower house. A commission for the inspection of nunneries was appointed; at Roxbury the members trampled all over a convent, looking into every closet and under every bed. They then regaled themselves, on a state expense account, with a champagne dinner, though the sale of intoxicants was forbidden by law. At the next election, the party was swept out of existence in Massachusetts, covered with ridicule.

A few Catholic publicists—in particular the celebrated Orestes Brownson—said truly enough that some of the immigrants would do well to mind their manners and be more respectful of American institutions, but nothing could disguise the fact that it was the Nativists themselves who had least regard for much that America stood for. It should be added that the country badly needed workmen, especially those willing to do the rough work on canals and railways and at the docks that other Americans usually managed to avoid. In short, the immigrants were not competing with the native-born, but were making an important contribution of their own to American prosperity.

With the redoubtable Bishop Hughes in New York, the Nativists could not get very far there. When they staged a demonstration in 1844 in the hope that it would provoke a Catholic attack, Hughes, contrary to expectations, forbade retaliation. Yet it should not be disguised that the policy of Hughes, and of other American bishops partly helped to occasion the Nativist outbursts. Those governing the Church thought that the immigrants should be encouraged to settle in cities where their spiritual needs could be looked after, instead of going to country districts where, in those days, few priests were to be found. German and other national groups went off to farm lands, where they formed homogeneous communities and were not molested.

The situation was this: many people landed in this country quite intending to continue in the United States the occupation of farming which had been theirs in Europe. It was only to earn money to travel further, and to buy and equip farms, that they remained—they usually imagined that it would be for only a short while—at the port at which they had entered. But it was in the cities that they found compatriots of their own gregarious kind, and formed roots from which they were seldom able to disentangle themselves. There, too, they found thriving Catholic churches and were assured that there were not many of these in the midwest. Even the priests who came from Europe were soon brought to believe that they were more needed in the East than anywhere else.

Some bishops did promote colonizing schemes, but usually

on too small a scale. The colony that Fenwick of Boston organized at Benedicta, Maine, is a case in point; it was very successful, as far as it went, but there should have been dozens more like it. Later colonizing projects, such as those promoted by Spalding of Peoria and Ireland of St. Paul came too late, and had inadequate financial resources. Such Irishmen who did settle on the land were usually those who, after laboring with pick and shovel on railway or canal, bought a small tract nearby.

The urbanization of the Irish was not due wholly to ecclesiastical policy, but to force of circumstances. Neverthless, it must be admitted that Hughes, an archbishop since 1850, seems to have gone out of his way to offer opposition to colonizing schemes. Once, a Father Tracy came to New York from Nebraska, hoping to persuade Irishmen to settle in that state. In the middle of one of his meetings a figure wearing an overcoat with its collar turned up, stood up in the gallery and roundly denounced the whole idea as poorly backed financially and badly managed. It was the archbishop. He also charged that D'Arcy McGee's schemes for colonization were not only chimerical but promoted in the interest of land speculators.

An incident closely connected with the Nativist uproar was the arrival in 1853 of Archbishop Bedini, the nuncio to Brazil, who bore a personal letter from the Pope to President Franklin Pierce, and who intended to investigate the advisability of sending a nuncio to the United States. Hughes, like other bishops, was opposed to this, as they feared that non-Catholic Americans might resent it. Bedini, though a pleasant sort of person, was violently objected to, roughly handled at Wheeling and Cincinnati, and was even in some danger of being lynched. Upon his departure he was advised not to take ship from the dock in New York, but to join it from a tug out of Staten Island. Hughes happened to be in Cuba just then, but he declared upon his return that had he been in

New York he would have taken Bedini to the docks in his own carriage, and was certain that no insult or display of violence would have occurred. As it was, a scare had been created, and the appointment of an apostolic delegate to the United States had to wait for forty years.

Hughes always said that he would take no part in politics, though one fancies that to so truculent a man this was a self-denying ordinance. He certainly refused, upon the conditions imposed, to act as a diplomatic agent during the war with Mexico; but during the Civil War, when his terms were met by the administration, he did go on a mission to France, with the result that that country's neutrality was obtained. This, however, was international diplomacy, not intervention in politics.

Even less so was what Hughes did in 1840 about the public-school issue. The public schools at that time were not as secularized as they are today; on the contrary, the tone that prevailed in them was definitely Protestant, yet Catholic children were obliged to attend them, for want of anything else. While Catholics were willing to co-operate with public schools, yet, as Hughes put it: "We are unwilling to pay taxes for the purpose of destroying our religion in the minds of our children." In this Hughes was supported by the Governor of New York, William H. Seward, as well as by other fair-minded Protestants.

The fight finally went against Catholics, necessitating the establishment of separate schools. In 1847, when he was invited to address Congress, his subject was "Christianity the only Source of Moral, Social and Political Regeneration," with the corollary that Catholicism, as the most conservative form of Christianity, was necessary to the perpetuation of free institutions. The thesis was a commonplace among Catholics, but to the members of Congress it probably seemed highly paradoxical. Nor were Catholic schools a novelty, though they could not often be founded; it is to John Hughes that the country owes most for the clarification of the controversy regarding public and parochial schools.

It was Archbishop Hughes who began the building of the present Cathedral of St. Patrick's—though it was completed by his successor McCloskey; and near it he went to live, leaving Mott Street for a residence on Madison Avenue, taking with him his sister, Mrs. Rodrigue, and her husband and children. At this time he had rather more social life than formerly, despite his failing health.

When the draft riots occurred, in July, 1863, he went out, ill though he was, to address the crowds, though most of those who heard him were law-abiding citizens and not rioters at all. The Irish, whether they fought in the armies of the North or the South, so greatly distinguished themselves as soldiers that special emissaries from both sides were sent to Ireland to spur recruiting. However, many who were ostensibly brought to these shores with a promise of good jobs were told upon their arrival that the jobs for which they had been hired were not yet quite ready and were by this device pressed into the army. These Irish immigrants not unnaturally felt, when they were drafted for military duty, that they had been tricked. Such being the case, some of them became highly skilled in "bounty jumping."

Other cities had draft riots, but it was to the rioters of New York that Archbishop Hughes appealed. Previously he had written in another connection what applied equally well at this time, words that indicate his feeling for the land of his birth as well as for the country of which he had long been a citizen: "Never forget your country; love her; defend her when the time comes; but let this love of old Ireland affect you only individually. In your social and political relations you must become merged in the country of your adoption." Now, speaking to the rioters, he showed something of his old fire and was twice called back to receive an ovation.

This was his last speech; his last sermon had been delivered in June, though in July he went to Baltimore for Archbishop Kenrick's funeral. He was then so weak that, when he attempted to say Mass, he almost fainted and had to be helped out of his vestments. During August and September he traveled in the hope of regaining his health but did not regain it. In December he was obliged to take to his bed, and about Christmas was told that his doctors said he would not recover. On the morning of January 3, 1864, Mass was said in his room, after which he began to sink, and early that evening he died.

Never very notable as a scholar, he was able to use to great effect whatever he knew, and probably more profundity would, in his case, have been hampering. Not a great preacher, he was nevertheless a forceful and lucid speaker. By sheer force of character and versatile ability, he was easily the most influential prelate of his time during the nearly forty years of his priesthood.

XII: Peter De Smet

(1801–1873)

It was the rather dour Belgian, Charles Nerinckx, who labored so devotedly in Kentucky who, when passing through Washington on his way to Europe, was asked by the Superior of the Jesuit missions to try and procure applicants for the Jesuit Order in the United States. While young Americans did now and then apply to be admitted, they often proved unsuited for the Jesuit manner of life. It seemed then that reliable recruits were to be obtained only from abroad. Nobody could have been a more zealous recruiting sergeant than Nerinckx. Among the eight men he gathered in Belgium in 1821 (he had obtained others in 1817) was Peter De Smet.

The group was under the direction of Fr. Charles Felix Van Quickenborne, who was appointed novice master, though he was only thirty-three, when they assembled at the Jesuit novitiate at White Marsh, Maryland. At the end of their two years there they set out for St. Louis. As Van Quickenborne said: "It was the Indian mission above everything else that brought us to Missouri and it is the principal point in the Concordat." They left for that little town—it was still far from deserving the name of city—on April 11, 1823. Bishop Dubourg was anxious to have them there. He already had a band of Vincentian priests, but these were engaged in a completely different field of work. Their route was by way of Baltimore, Frederick, and Cumberland to Wheeling, West Virginia. There they obtained two flat-boats, which they lashed together, on one of them placing a wagon and their stock of provisions. At Louisville they were met by Nerinckx, and a pilot was engaged to get them safely over the falls. In this way they went down the Ohio as far as Shawneetown, where they disembarked. Sending their baggage to St. Louis by steamboat, they themselves, to save time, went across country, reaching that settlement on May 30, 1823. The journey had taken seven weeks.

Peter De Smet completed his studies at St. Louis and was ordained there, with several other young Jesuits, on September 23, 1827. Then, as is the Jesuit custom, he spent a full year devoted to spiritual activities, after which he was sent to conduct a small Indian school at Florisant, Missouri.

Two points about this undertaking are of special interest. St. Regis Academy was the first missionary enterprise undertaken anywhere in the world by the Jesuits since their restoration. Second, it received financial aid from the federal government through the good offices of William Clark, of Lewis and Clark fame.

John C. Calhoun, Secretary of War under President Monroe and in whose department then fell the direction of Indian affairs (though a separate bureau was later established), arranged that a subsidy of $200 a year was to be paid for each missionary to the Indians and also that Washington would contribute towards the erection of buildings to house the missionaries. This subsidy was at first given to only three men, then to four. Furthermore, an appropriation of $800 a year was made towards the support of Indian boys at the school that was set up, an appropriation later raised to $1,900. Calhoun even offered a Jesuit, Father Levins, who was a mathematician of some note, a professorship at West Point. It is evident that the principle of the separation of Church and State was still accepted in the sense intended by the Founding Fathers as the co-operation of the federal government with religious enterprises. This principle still prevails in the case of those working among the Indians.

In 1841 Father De Smet told a cousin of Prince Gallitzin,

who was the visitator of the Religious of the Sacred Heart: "Believe me, you will never succeed in this country till you draw down on your work the blessing of God by founding an establishment among the savages." Mother Gallitzin answered that this was just what their superior general wished. "But," she went on, "we have neither subjects nor money." De Smet replied: "Still, you must do it." To this prodding of his we must attribute the actual start of missionary work among the Indians on the part of these nuns.

Mother Gallitzin was well aware that she had at hand one religious who had come to America in 1818 specifically for this purpose, but who had been deflected from it by founding boarding schools for the daughters of white settlers at St. Louis and several other points down the Mississippi. The schools conducted by this religious institute are unquestionably among the best of their kind in this country, yet few people are aware that it was not to found schools but to convert the Indians that the Religious of the Sacred Heart came to this country.

Long before this conversation, Philippine Duchesne—the nun who was in command of this group—had cherished for at least ten years before she actually arrived in America the project of going there to work among the Indians. But this ambition had to be laid aside because Mother Madeleine Sophie Barat could not spare Philippine, who was her right hand in their work in France. It was only the arrival at their Paris house of Bishop Dubourg of St. Louis, who was seeking nuns for America, that gave Philippine the chance she was quick to seize. When the bishop was saying good-bye, she thought, "Now or never!" and fell at Mother Barat's feet, crying: "If only I could go, I would be willing even to be superior." Such a conjuration the tender-hearted superior general found it impossible to refuse.

Superior she had to be, and as such she saw that her immediate duty was the founding of schools. At the time there were no Catholic schools for girls nearer to St. Louis than New Orleans, a thousand miles down the Mississippi, and one or two to the east in Kentucky. These first schools conducted by the Religious of the Sacred Heart were for many years so poverty-stricken that Philippine could not feel free to go to the Indians until her establishments had reached a reasonable degree of prosperity and stability.

The fees charged had to be absurdly low—they were that everywhere in those days—and often enough the fees were not paid. Had it not been that the nuns came from fairly wealthy French families, they could not have been maintained at all.

Mother Duchesne labored heroically as superior, but always regarded herself as so inefficient in that position that she frequently begged Mother Barat to replace her. Indeed, she could not have been of much use as a teacher because of her inability to learn English; she was even to write her superior general of "the nothingness of my works and emptiness of my heart." Yet she had to remain as superior until she was over seventy. Then, when Mother Gallitzin arrived as visitator, Philippine's resignation was accepted, and it was decided that she might go to the Potawatomi Indian settlement at Sugar Creek, Kansas.

She and the nuns with her, when at last they reached Sugar Creek, were received by 150 Potawatomi braves riding at full tilt in all their feathered regalia. By the end of the day in the settlement poor Philippine's right hand was almost pulp after she had shaken hands with 700 Indian men, after which she submitted, very joyfully, to being embraced by their squaws.

The Indians deeply venerated her as "the woman who always prays" and would creep up to her to touch her habit as she knelt absorbed before the Blessed Sacrament. But except for what her evident holiness effected, she was of little practical use as a missionary, as she never learned more than a word or two of the gutteral Potawatomi. Again she tasted, and this time even more bitterly, what she regarded as failure.

Though Mother Gallitzin said: "If she cannot work, she will forward the success of the missions by her prayers," the hardship of living in a wigwam, where she slept on the bare ground, was a bit too much for one so old. Moreover, when winter arrived she had to go through deep snow to reach the chapel, where she spent most of her time, and it became clear that, indomitable though she was, she could not long support this mode of life. When Peter Richard Kenrick, then coadjutor to Bishop Rosati of St. Louis, arrived at the Indian settlement and saw the state of affairs, he at once ordered her return. Philippine sadly recognized the wisdom of this decision, and accepted it. But at St. Charles there was not much that she could do except pray. There she lingered on until November 12, 1852, when she died at the age of eighty-three. She was beatified in 1940.

The Religious of the Sacred Heart, soon after their arrival, had taken several Indian girls into their schools, but they wished to set up a school specially for Indians, planning to take from forty to sixty; and as they had some money of their own and received contributions from pious associations, they asked only for a subsidy of $800 a year from the federal government. The idea was that the boys whom the Jesuits were educating at Florissant would need Christian wives if they were to be prevented from relapsing into savagery. All this, of course, was part of the effort to civilize the tribes, and that it was welcomed by the Indians themselves is indicated by the arrival at St. Louis in September, 1823, of a deputation from six tribes which was on its way to Washington to arrange a confederacy under government auspices. They proposed exchanging their lands east of the Mississippi for reservations in the Indian Territory.

In 1840 the Indian project was further extended by the appointment of Nicholas Point as a missionary to the Indian tribes in Kansas, while De Smet went on a prospecting tour of the Rocky Mountain regions. De Smet and another Jesuit had been working since 1838 at Council Bluffs and elsewhere in what was known as the Platte Purchase, and in January, 1837, Van Quickenborne had visited the Potawatomi in their encampment opposite Fort Leavenworth.

Van Quickenborne, while he baptized a fairly large number of Indian children, made few converts among the adults, though we hear of his marrying an Indian couple on May 13, 1837. He had not been very optimistic when he wrote two years previously to the General of the Jesuits that the "Indians were not to be converted except by men who could work miracles." Such men were, as we know, found; and the conversion of the Indians would not have been very difficult had it not been for their weakness for fire-water. As Father Verreydt wrote from Council Bluff in a letter in 1841: "Getting drunk is the only fault they have; otherwise we would live here in Paradise." We have some almost unbelievable accounts of the maddening effects of whiskey upon the Indians, De Smet writing in July, 1839, to a nun at Termonde, Belgium, telling of fourteen murders committed by drunken men, one of whom seized his own child by the legs and crushed its head against the post of his lodge—and that in the presence of the horrified mother. "The passion of the savages for strong drink is incredible," he writes. "They give horses, blankets, all, in a word, to have a little of this brutalizing drink." He looked for better fortune among the Flatheads of Oregon, to whom he went in 1840.

The blackrobes who worked among the tribes of the Great Plains said wonderingly of their converts that many of them were so devout that it was like seeing the Christians of the time of the Apostles; often, after a whole series of confessions, they declared that they could find nothing that called for absolution. It was much the same when some years earlier Bishop Bruté met at a place near the present University of Notre Dame the Potawatomi who had come there from the neighborhood of Detroit, where they had been under the care of Père Richard. The Bishop rode among them, with a half-breed named Catherine Campau as interpreter and the priest who accompanied them, Fr. Deseilles. He learned that many of them—some of them children only ten years old—fasted for several days in preparation for their first Communion. Upon these and others he administered confirmation before they departed, escorted by a regiment of American soldiers headed by General Tipton, on their enforced migration across the Mississippi. One of Bruté's priests, —whom he would like to have had as his coadjutor—the Jesuit Fr. Petit was asked to go along, but he and the bishop at first declined, lest this might seem to implicate the Church in an action they both deplored. They changed their minds only because they did not wish the Potawatomi to be without spiritual aid on their long trek.

Then a report reached Washington that Petit had tried to persuade the Indians to resist deportation, upon which the $300 appropriation Petit had been receiving was stopped. Only after some correspondence with the Commissioner for Indian Affairs was the appropriation renewed, and increased —perhaps in reparation—to $400. The commissioner also undertook to pay for the erection of some buildings for the Indians—the chief of these a chapel and a house for the missionary—out of what was called the civilization fund. For these buildings and a school house the amount paid over was $2,000.

Three churches were eventually built for this tribe, all of them small. At the opening of the third church, "a neat and spacious structure" forty feet long and twenty feet wide, a rifle was fired at the door, to meet with the response of 300 others, fired by the braves at the doors of their cabins. Though schools for the Indians were established, Catholics received so small a portion of the government appropriation that in 1836, out of fifty-two schools, only three were conducted by Catholics, the Methodists and Baptists getting the lion's share of official support—this though it was Catholics who were by far the most active missionaries. And however it may have been with subsidies paid to other denominations, the Catholic subsidies usually arrived late. But the money did come in eventually and was of great assistance.

The federal government rarely observed the treaties it made with the Indians, and these were often obtained by making the council of chiefs drunk so that they did not fully understand what they were signing, and were often shamefully swindled. This was especially true after the Civil War, when hundreds of former soldiers were compensated with Indian lands for the services they had rendered to the cause of the North. This may perhaps be defended on the grounds that the Indians thriftlessly did little to cultivate their fertile acres. Such a defense is rather lame when it is recalled that the treaty of 1825 with the Osage guaranteed their unmolested possession of their reserve "as long as the grass grows on the plains and water continues to flow down the Missouri"; in spite of which a commission was sent to them to demand the surrender of their lands. Realizing that the white settlers were determined to have their way, the priests advised the Indians to give back those holdings which were not in actual use. The Osage thus ceded about a million acres for $300,000, as well as another tract three times as large, which was to be sold for a dollar and a quarter an acre, the money received to be kept by the government in trust for the tribe. Even of this they were, for the most part, defrauded.

It was a standing grievance with the Indians, in particular the Arapaho and the Cheyenne, that, when they had expected Catholic missionaries, Protestants were sent to them. While this may sometimes have been because of a misunderstanding, yet when the Cheyenne sent a delegation to Washington that made it quite clear that only Jesuits were wanted, nothing was done. Under President Grant the policy was announced of giving support to "such denominations as had previously established themselves among the Indians." This would have been satisfactory, had it been honestly carried out, for Catholic priests were the first to go as missionaries. But ways and means were found for avoiding the federal law.

De Smet's personal, direct and active period as a missionary did not last much more than ten years, and during a good deal of that time he was making extensive trips in the United States and Europe to raise funds for his work. Perhaps it was his success in this work that resulted in his appointment as provincial procurator. The position was meant to be only temporary, but De Smet showed so much accurate, industry and minute attention to detail—which were remarkable in a man whose previous occupations had not seemed to be an adequate training for business—that he never obtained release from his new duties. He did, however, keep in constant touch with the missions, visiting them as often as he could, and several times being used by the government as intermediary between them and the Indians.

His guiding principle as procurator seemed to be to save as much as possible, by the exercise of care and economy, for missionary work. From the administration in Washington he obtained an allowance of $50 a year for the education of each Indian boy or girl in Jesuit schools. This worked out, he said, to fourteen cents a day—which had to cover tuition, clothing, washing and mending, stationery and books. This allowance was later raised to $75, which was still quite inadequate. De Smet was able to keep the missions going at all only by the appeals he made to charitable people. During the years when he had traveled in search of funds, his fame was so great, his personality so compelling, that he could freely approach even the very great personages in his rusty frock coat (from which a button or two might be missing).

In the Indian schools the rule had to be that the boys were to work in the fields during the summer and study the rest of the year. This was not easy to effect, as the Indians thought of such work as something that only women performed. In the task of overseeing the manual work, and even that of the classroom, the lay brothers, a holy and devoted set of men who were more numerous than the priests, shouldered much of the responsibility. The priests worked in the fields, too, and gave the courses in religious instruction.

Some of the early Jesuit priests deserve a particular word or two. Maurice Gaillant, a Swiss, ministered to the sick with positive gaiety. After giving the last sacraments he would exclaim: "Well, *he* is ripe for heaven; now I am ready for somebody else." And if he saw an Indian loitering about the church he would say to him: "Don't you want to go to confession? I have a little time now."

Christian Hoecken, Superior of St. Mary's College, Kansas, was a famous preacher. In his mouth Potawatomi is said to have sounded "as mellifluous and liquid as the softest Greek or Italian." He preached a sermon to a group of Indians who had gathered at Notre Dame University, and the description was: "There was from beginning to end an uninterrupted torrent of speech that reminded the listeners of the eloquence of Ulysses whose hurrying words Homer compares to the countless flakes of snow in the wintry storm."

John Baptist Miége, after being Bishop of the Indian Territory, and founding what was to be Detroit University, ended his days as spiritual director at Woodstock College. He had twice sought to be relieved of his office: in 1863, and again in 1868, when he saw how the Indians were being driven out by the tide of incoming whites.

But this general account of missionary work among the Indians has deflected some of the attention that should be given to Peter De Smet. It may be that he lay under an illusion in thinking that the Flatheads might form a new Paraguay;

the Reductions of the seventeenth century would not have been possible in nineteenth-century America. It was with sorrow that De Smet became aware of the rich mineral deposits in the mountains of the West, as he knew that there would be such a rush to exploit them that the Perce Nez, the Coeur d'Alenes and the other tribes would be roughly ejected by the incoming whites. He was perhaps the best friend the Indians ever had; as Chittenden and Richardson say in their voluminous account of him: he was "an august figure in our national history," and again: "The history of the native races of North America can never be written without consulting the writings of Father De Smet."

Short, stocky and rather corpulent, with a wide and always smiling mouth, he almost became an Indian himself, little as he was one in appearance. His capacious stomach sometimes enabled him to attend as many as twenty Indian feasts in a single day, much to the approval of his hosts. He even came to enjoy—or said that he did—the dog flesh served at their banquets. Best of all, the Indians set him down as the one white man they had ever known who did not speak with a double tongue.

This was immense service in composing inter-tribal wars as well as outbreaks against the whites, and the federal government was only too glad to avail itself of his good offices, knowing that the Indians completely trusted him. Over and over again he had proved to the Indians his devoted concern, as when a colonel of militia ordered a massacre of several hundred Indians—women and children among them—who had come, according to their custom, to make a friendly visit to the fort he commanded. "Still," wrote De Smet, "the monster found admirers and defenders, and still wears his epaulets."

That is why this Jesuit priest was able to do what no other white man could have done, go alone and unarmed in 1868 into the camp of the Sioux at the time of the famous Sitting

Bull. A speech made in Congress called this one of the most remarkable achievements in the history of our Indian wars, and the commissioners acknowledged that, but for De Smet, their work would have been a failure. It is true that the peace did not last long and that in 1876 the Sioux under Sitting Bull exterminated General Custer's force, but the peace might have been kept had not the whites continued to give provocation to a race constitutionally suspicious.

It is told how during one of his visits to the Sioux De Smet awoke one night to see a young brave standing over him with a drawn dagger. "Are you not afraid, Blackrobe?" the Indian asked, when De Smet opened calm eyes. For answer De Smet took the man's hand and held it over his heart. There was not the slightest tremor. De Smet was absolutely fearless, as well as absolutely honest.

His main work was done between 1840 and 1846 among the Indians of the Rocky Mountain region, and he really had a good deal more to do with saving Oregon for the union than ever Dr. Marcus Whitman did. Though the doctor did make his celebrated ride, it is a sheer myth that it had a patriotic object; it was to avert the closing down of the Oregon missions by the society that had started them. De Smet, however, like the two Canadians sent into those regions as bishops—Augustine and Francis Blanchet—did not meddle in politics. He did all he could, however, as did Dr. John A. McLoughlin, the agent of the Hudson Bay Company, who became a Catholic, by trying to keep relations friendly between the new American settlers and the Indians. They helped to make the passage into the hands of the United States easy when its claim to Oregon was put forward in 1846.

When De Smet first set out for distant Oregon in 1840, he has as his guide Jean-Baptist de Velder, an old grenadier who had served under the Emperor Napoleon. Setting out from St. Louis in April, it was July before they reached the camp of the Flatheads and the Pend d'Oreilles. His work was done among them and the other mountain tribes, though he was frequently absent, pressing deep into Canada, or going to New Orleans and Philadelphia, the cities most generous in giving him donations, or traveling to Europe itself for funds. He also visited Washington frequently, because of the business he had to transact with the officials in whose charge the Indians lived.

It seems a pity that so effectual a go-between of the Jesuits and the federal government should during his last years have been largely occupied with his procuratorship instead of being allowed to continue among the Indians, which was the main reason, after all, why the Jesuits had gone to St. Louis. Though De Smet never lost sight of this work, his opportunities to be of assistance were more and more restricted to times of crisis when only he could be of service. He no doubt would never have become what Fr. Gilbert Garraghan calls a "typical missionary," for his energetic and, indeed, somewhat restless disposition would have often sent him out on long journeys to stir up interest in what was being done. Fr. John Rothensteiner gives a clear and just summary of this work: "Had the Jesuit missionaries of the West been allowed to pursue their plans without let or hindrance, or, better still, had they received the undivided support of the government in the work of Christianization, these numerous and once powerful tribes would now form large and prosperous communities on our Western prairies. But Catholic efforts were not supported as they should have been, nay, were often hampered by government rules under some specious plea or other. Our Catholic people, too, were not as earnest in this great work as might have been expected of them."

It is probable enough that American Catholic interest would have been much increased if De Smet had been allowed to go more often to the populous centres in the East, and he might even have been able to do a good deal more to obtain fairer treatment for the Indians at Washington. But even

De Smet did not have the strength to change the too universal frame of mind of the white men, whose declared principle was that the only good Indian was a dead Indian. The surge of the white settlers westwards was irresistible. Therefore, the tribes were cooped up in reservations—tracts of land considered of little use—and there they live disconsolately, believing in their heart of hearts that their way of life was superior to much that is found among men who are supposed to be civilized. Many of them are Catholics, but usually in a somewhat listless way, as compared with the fervor the early missionaries often encountered. Sadly it must be said that, bright as De Smet's personal glory still shines, his was a dream that to a great extent has been allowed to fade.

XIII: Orestes Brownson

(1803–1876)

Whether Orestes Brownson was the greatest and most luminous mind produced by American Catholicism, as many believe, he surely was one of the most rugged and forceful of personalities, as also of an unpredictable eccentricity that colors, if not always charms, all that he did and said. Without pretending to be a Brownsonian—for such people are often too earnest and solemn in their admiration for his philosophy—I am Brownsonian at least in the sense that I delight in this forthright, booming, table-thumping man.

Brownson was born in the little village of Stockbridge, Vermont, and to the end of his days he was intensely proud of the fact that he was a Vermonter, unmistakably a product of the rocky hills of his native state. His father having died when he was young, and his widow being too poor to support her children, Orestes and his two brothers and two sisters were given into the charge of various families, and saw each other and their mother only rarely. With the elderly couple with whom he was placed he inevitably acquired, while still a boy, something of the behavior of an old man. Having no playmates, he avidly read whatever books he could find, one of them by Jonathan Edwards. The theology of that writer is about as uncompromising as it is possible to be, but that may have been providential in Brownson's case, as providing a lever for recoil. It might also be remarked that the clear and delicate style of that grim theologian, led him, without his setting out to find it, to an excellent prose style of his own.

When Orestes was fourteen, Mrs. Brownson moved to

Ballston Spa, then a fashionable resort north of Albany, and she was able to gather her children together and provide a home, as the little that her sons could earn at least made family life possible. A year or two later Orestes was able to attend a fairly good school in the village and acquired enough learning to become a school teacher himself for a while. Henry Brownson may be correct in saying that his father studied Latin and Greek; if so, he got of Greek the merest smattering, and the Latin he found he needed in due time, like everything else he learned, was almost entirely self-taught.

At that time he underwent the experience known as conversion (as understood by what are called "evangelical" Protestants) and became a Presbyterian, his foster parents having been only vaguely and nominally Congregationalists, who seldom went to church. But Brownson, whose mind was already full of philosophical and theological speculations, to which—naturally enough in the case of a youth quite untrained—he could find no conclusions, described his joining the Presbyterians as "the act of an intellectual desperado." These Presbyterians were strict Calvinists, but, perhaps because of his reading of Jonathan Edwards, he swallowed their doctrines without question. Indeed, though the exercise of his intelligence soon obliged him to discard their formal tenets, there remained upon him for a long while—and perhaps to the end of his life—some of the marks of ingrained Puritanism. Yet his logical mind already led him to see that, if Christ really did found a Church, it could be no other than the Catholic Church. "But that Church," he added, in his account of his early life, seemed out of the question; "It was everything that was vile, base, odious, and demoralizing."

The dilemma between inescapable reason and what he then believed to be historical fact was torturing. He was sure he could no longer remain a Presbyterian; his reaction against Calvinism was so strong that he escaped by turning a Universalist. As he wished to be in a new place, he went to

Detroit, where he knew nobody, and where he hoped he would be able to think out his problems in quiet. In that little town of hardly more than a thousand inhabitants he was ordained a Universalist minister at the age of twenty-three. With that his dizzy, breath-taking career began.

He occupied—always for rather brief periods—several Universalist pulpits in New Hampshire, Vermont and New York, and must have made some mark, as would be indicated by his being asked to edit the magazine of that denomination. Yet he was no better satisfied with this new group than he had been with the Presbyterians. He was forever asking questions to which there was no answer, so he tried to occupy his mind and to find an outlet for his superabundant energies in Sociology and politics.

Oddly enough, the liberating agent was the eccentric but engaging Fanny Wright. She was of a class of reformers of whom America was rather full. A young Englishwoman of some means, and the adopted daughter of Lafayette, she was socially very acceptable. Disregarding all that (and quite indifferent to the lurid colors in which she was pictured by some journalists with a keen nose for a sensational story, who represented her as a kind of Jezebel because she professed to believe in free love, though she never practiced it), what she was really interested in was the establishment in Tennessee of a colony in which slaves could buy their freedom by a stated term of labor.

She was a fairly good-looking person and a good public speaker. Brownson was captivated. The relations between the two were completely innocent, for they were brought together by their absorbed discussion of social questions, in which both took an extremely radical line. Brownson always spoke kindly of Fanny, and greatly admired her oratorical gifts. When she married a Frenchman who—as was then possible under existing French law—appropriated her fortune, leaving her to die impoverished and forgotten, Brownson was rightly indignant at the treatment she had received. Long before getting acquainted with her, he had himself married, and was an irreproachable if somewhat stormy husband. There is not the slightest reason to believe that his wife was in the least jealous of Fanny; she was too sensible and knew her husband too well.

We find Brownson about this time associated with the short-lived Workingmen's Party—Arthur M. Schlesinger, Jr., has gone so far as to call him a forerunner of Karl Marx—and then supporting William H. Seward, the Jacksonian candidate for the governorship of New York. In each instance he acted as a freelance; it never occurred to him to seek political office for himself. Even when he became a Catholic he was addicted to springing his private crochets upon people, still without seeking personal profit or advancement. However, the idiosyncrasy of some of his ideas, and even more the philosophical system that he concocted, made many Catholics eye him a bit askance. To anticipate matters a little, the extravagance of several of his early notions, and the belligerence with which he defended them, was a convenient excuse for his transcendentalist friends dropping him, when he added to his former divagations the absurdity (as they thought it) of Catholicism.

Yet it is only fair to say that the transcendentalist friends had some justification. Presbyterian, Universalist and Unitarian in quick succession, and then in Boston founding his own "Church of the Future," it is hardly to be wondered at that he had acquired a reputation of instability. To Lowell in his *Fable for Critics* he was "weathercock Brownson," and none of his friends—Theodore Parker, Emerson, Alcott, Ripley and Bradford of Brook Farm, and young Thoreau, to whom he taught a little of his self-taught German—could believe that so intelligent a man could possibly remain a Catholic for long. They would not have been surprised had he become a Buddhist, except that he did not have the temperament for that. In the end he would no doubt become a transcendentalist like themselves—indeed, he had been on the fringe of the movement for some time without dissolving into its nebulosity—but that would come; surely, there was nothing else that could happen. When they discovered that he really was firmly rooted at last, they could not understand it and gave him up. So have most of the later critics of American literature.

He had for a good many years been strenuously educating himself, at least to the extent of acquiring a good reading knowledge of the languages used by the foreign philosophers he needed to master—Benjamin Constant, Cousin, Leroux, Rosmini, Jouffroy and others. From them he derived many of his ideas, yet what he presented was not a mere patchwork or synthesis but a system which, while he was constantly modifying it, was transformed and made original. The main theory upon which he harped a good deal was what he styled "communionism," and this eventually led him to the Catholic Church; this had nothing to do with communism. To give Brownson's own definition, communionism was "the doctrine that man lives by communion with man, and through the life derived from Jesus with God, which will bring us on one platform, in the unity of life itself, and the Church will become one in Christ."

That theory is not far from Catholic doctrine, but, instead of leading him directly to the Church, it inspired his attempt to create what he called the Church of the Future. As this in some respects was not very different from some forms of Unitarianism, Brownson frequently preached at the church of the celebrated Dr. William Ellery Channing, a man who during this period was a kind of father confessor to him, in the sense that Brownson confided to him the working of his mind.

The tall gaunt Vermonter would arrive at Channing's rooms in a frock coat and a high hat, with a cargo of books under his arm and a wad of tobacco in his cheek. As he was already a mighty trencherman, he would slip out after the meagre lunch that Channing provided to get a square meal at a hotel by way of stoking up for the second (the evening) sermon. As to how much the congregation really understood of what he said may be a question; there is no question at all that they were interested. To everybody it was evident that here was an absolutely sincere man, and one of great originality.

It was much the same when he visited Brook Farm, a project which he had helped inspire, but with which he had no definite connection. Young Isaac Hecker was there, and had gone because Brownson advised it. The two men talked of nothing but religion, and to the other farmers who heard Brownson's booming voice it was evident that both of them had their faces turned towards Rome. Many of these sensitive and idealistic people found that Brownson got on their nerves at times. But they were vastly entertained by a story that George Bradford told about him. It seems that one night he had a dream in which he was confessing his sins to "Fr. Brownson." When he ended their recital he was told: "Now for your penance say this psalm in Latin after me." Upon this, poor Bradford—an exquisite Latinist—awoke with horror at the thought of the false quantities he might expect from the self-educated Brownson, and groaned, like Cain: "O Lord, my punishment is greater than I can bear."

However, several of the Brook Farmers besides Hecker eventually became Catholics—for instance Mrs. Ripley. Others merely played with Catholicism. Hecker says that none of them grasped that the Church was a great deal more than a social institution.

Brownson aired his views in his *Boston Quarterly,* one of several magazines he had edited, and Catholics noticed the trend of his thought and were hardly surprised when Brownson not long afterwards called upon Bishop Fenwick, asking for admission into the Church. Fenwick turned him over to his coadjutor Fitzpatrick, though he was somewhat prejudiced against Brownson as a man who was "proud and conceited." Brownson found Fitzpatrick a little hard to talk to, as his mind constantly flickered back and forth between principles and witticisms. Hecker calls him, perhaps not quite justly, "the hierarchical exponent of all that was traditional and commonplace in Catholic public life." The point of that remark is that the formal kind of training the coadjutor had received at Montreal and Paris among the Sulpicians made him (not unnaturally) a bit distrustful of his catechumen's individualistic methods of controversy, as exemplified in his *Boston Quarterly*. Accordingly, he pressed the strict scholastic mode upon him, with the result that Brownson, who was already strong in logic, emerged as a logician and almost nothing else. While Brownson retained a strong personal flavor, he was to this extent deflected from the kind of apostolate he might have exercised, had he only been left to his devices.

Fitzpatrick, of course, could not cure Brownson of his truculence, and maybe he did not wish to cure him of that, though he may not have quite approved of all the ways it manifested itself, as these often exceeded the zeal commonly shown by converts. To offer one example: Brownson was at the inn at Andover, Massachusetts, sitting at the long common table of those days, when the landlord put before him the meat he provided all his guests. Brownson called him over and said he did not want it. Upon this the landlord asked if he could bring something else—perhaps a nice steak? Brownson roared so that the table rattled: "Don't you know that a Christian doesn't eat meat on Friday?" How should the poor man have known? Catholics had hardly ever been seen in that remote little village.

Brownson did much the same sort of thing in his controversies—and after his conversion most of these were with fellow Catholics. The freedom of the period was such that several times he got into arguments, either in his *Review* or by private correspondence, with members of the hierarchy. Even with them Brownson presented his case with great vigor, and not always with the tact or politeness one might have expected. In argument with less exalted people Brownson would, so to speak, bellow at the top of his voice and crash his huge fist down on the table, taking it for granted that his opponent would do the same, as he considered this the normal way of having a discussion. What Brownson failed to realize was his own strength; sometimes his blunt speech was good-humoredly accepted (it almost always was by people who knew his propensities), but, not infrequently, others were hurt and offended. What he had intended to be merely a friendly tap fell with such force that a bone was broken, a skull split. He rarely used a subtle rapier; usually it was a fearsome club. To get into an argument with Brownson was like wrestling with a bear.

An instance of this was when he severely criticized a book by Walter Hill, a Jesuit of the Western province who had some reputation as a philosopher. Fr. Hill used a stereotyped method, and later he wrote to Brownson confessing, "I don't pretend to be a philosopher; I only try to repeat what I was taught as a student." So modest an admission was disarming, but when he tried to be lofty with Brownson he was jumped on. When Brownson tried to show the unsoundness of one of Hill's points, the Jesuit said that the criticism must be due to Brownson's imperfect knowledge of scholastic Latin. Brownson accordingly wrote crushingly in his *Review*: "Though we find no difficulty in understanding the author when he explains his meaning in Latin, which we are said to be ignorant of, we have no little difficulty in getting at his meaning when he expresses it in English . . . Fr. Hill's English is far less intelligible to us than any scholastic Latin we ever encountered."

But that only concerned an individual Jesuit. It was much worse when Brownson said, and most emphatically, that the Jesuit system of education was inadequate for the age, that it did not take into sufficient account that modern society was full of varieties of opinion, and that an effort should be made to become *au courant* with these, as otherwise it would be impossible to do more than preach to those already converted. With this criticism it is no wonder that the Jesuits were seriously offended. Edward Gibbon (though he did not always observe his own wise maxim) warned against ever attacking institutions; the individual may get over his ruffled feelings—in any event, he dies in due course—whereas an institution, having continuous life, never forgets or forgives. Brownson's son Henry, who had unsuccessfully tried his vocation as a Jesuit, admitted that his father made a serious mistake in attacking the order. Yet, though some influential Jesuits may have become hostile, Brownson had Jesuit friends, notably, Father Augustus Thébaud.

Brownson also succeeded in offending the Irish, a race somewhat quick to take offense, and, because of their command of the resources of English, well able to strike back. Brownson had many Irish friends—indeed, the majority of his friends were Irish—but he touched the American Irish at a very sore point. When the Nativists were in their heyday—and most of their violence was directed against the Irish immigrants—Brownson, while deploring what had occurred, said bluntly that it would be well if the newcomers showed themselves more respectful towards American manners and modes of thought. This may have been true of a few of them, but was certainly not generally applicable.

Remarks of this sort cost him very dear. The future Cardinal Newman, whom he had also criticized very freely, but who did not bear any grudge, conceived that his critic was an extremely able man. So in 1853, when he was assembling a faculty for the university he was to head in Dublin, he wrote to Brownson, saying that he was the first man to be approached, inviting him to join the enterprise. He even suggested that Brownson live with him in Ireland. It was a most magnanimous offer which Brownson would have been very glad to accept, especially since Newman told him to pick any chair that he liked except for those in theology and metaphysics, as they would have to be reserved for ecclesiastics.

Alas, the Irish bishops—who had not taken kindly to an Englishman, of however great an eminence heading their Catholic University—objected to Brownson. They considered that he had shown himself anti-Irish in his remarks about Nativism. In face of that, Newman was obliged to write to Brownson again in August, 1854, asking him whether it would be "inconvenient" for him to "postpone" his visit, "on the ground of some offense which happens to be taken *just now* in America, and I believe in Ireland, at something you have lately written." To this Brownson, who understood better than Newman what was the trouble, answered that instead of postponing the matter, he had better decline the handsome offer. "I assure you," he told Newman "that the Irish party . . . have always disliked me, and will never accept me." It was his own fault, but he was greatly disappointed to have lost so grand a chance.

Sometimes, however, Brownson was himself attacked, and not at all fairly. Thus, in 1845 he had transferred himself and his magazine, renamed *Brownson's Review,* to New York at the definite invitation of Bishop Hughes. For a while all went fairly smoothly, but when in 1856 there came an invitation from St. John's College, the nucleus of the present Fordham University to give the commencement address, Hughes sat beside him on the platform. And though, when Brownson resumed his seat, the archbishop complimented him upon his speech, he concluded the ceremonies by launching into a reproof of Brownson. Brownson had said that if the

Catholic religion were presented to the American people "under auspices more congenial with the national feeling and habits" its "progress would be much greater." In a letter Hughes told Brownson: "This is pure speculation. But it is a view in which I do not and cannot concur." In his estimate of the question Hughes may have been quite right, but it would have been better if the beginnings of their difference had not been aired in public.

Brownson lost no time in transferring himself and *Brownson's Review* to Elizabeth, New Jersey, in the Newark diocese, under Bishop James Roosevelt Bayley. As the latter was himself a convert, he might prove more sympathetic than Hughes. Brownson knew that there was no sense in getting at further loggerheads with the redoubtable Bishop of New York. It is rather amusing to record that a bronze bust of Brownson (one that does not look much like him, depicting only a bearded and benign old gentleman) now stands in front of the Fordham University church. It must have been close to that spot that the Hughes-Brownson incident occurred.

From his safe retreat in Elizabeth the editor of *Brownson's Review* continued to fire his big guns in all directions. Every issue was written by the editor himself, and, though its circulation was not very large, it had great influence. In those days a magazine could be run for very little, especially when there were no contributors to pay. Brownson was paid when he wrote for the *Catholic World,* as he frequently did, so with this and an occasional lecture—for one of which the sale of tickets brought him in a thousand dollars—he managed well enough. Then, too, a group of his admirers gave him an annual pension of another thousand. He had all he wanted for his needs.

In his *Review* there were many long polemical articles, and in it, too, he often used material subsequently published in book form. In it appeared his autobiography *The Convert,* an excellent account of the intellectual cross-currents he encountered before he became a Catholic. In his novel, *The Spirit-Rapper,* several of the leading transcendentalists are recognizable characters, along with the spiritualists, the Fox Sisters, but the work is hardly a shining example of the novelist's art. However, his study of political philosophy, *The American Republic,* was very brilliant, and is a most searching and profound analysis of the subject, with special relation to the issues that brought about the Civil War.

As a literary critic Brownson is still well worth reading, though some of his judgments make one gasp a bit. Thus, he thought *The Scarlet Letter* immoral and decided that Emerson's poems, even while he admitted their beauty, were really "hymns to the devil." Yet, upon the whole, he did excellent service by instantly exposing pretentious humbug. And members of the hierarchy who set up shop as authors were never safe from his barbs if he found anything in their books that in his opinion was insecurely based upon historical fact, though such works received the compliment of close and careful examination.

After the death of his wife, their daughter Sarah was in charge of his household, and she was too much like her father to get on with him very well. Sarah was appalled, now that it was she who paid the bills, at the enormous quantity of meat that the gouty old man consumed. Then, too, she seems to have been of a somewhat suspicious nature, for whenever she heard her father laughing with the seamstress who came to the house, or one of the maids, she imagined a flirtation, or even that a second marriage was in the offing. She married when she was forty, but Brownson, after living awhile with Sarah and her husband, and finding that the arrangement was not going to work, moved to the house of his son Henry, a Detroit lawyer. His daughter-in-law Fifine was a special favorite of his, perhaps because she better understood how to handle the ailing, corpulent, crochetty old man. Of Fifine's children, too, he was fond; as he was, for that matter, of

Sarah's. And it is pleasant to record that, at long range, the somewhat acerbated feelings of father and daughter mellowed, and that peace was restored. There had never ceased to be love underneath the acrimonious complaints made on both sides.

On Good Friday, 1876, Brownson and his son had a beautiful blusterous argument—on a theological point, of course. By midnight he was seriously ill, so that he had to receive the last sacraments on Holy Saturday. At dawn on Easter Sunday he died, being buried first in Detroit but afterwards in the crypt of the church of Notre Dame University. As he lies there in the centre of the aisle—and the crypt is used almost as much as the main church above it—scores of young men walk every morning on their way to receive Holy Communion over the slab that covers the grave in which lie the bones of Orestes Brownson.

XIV: Samuel Mazzuchelli

(1806–1864)

This extraordinary pioneer priest—a very attractive personality, as well as a man of enormous energy and versatility and absolute devotedness—was born in Milan of a family that had been there since the time of St. Ambrose. They were highly cultivated and pious, though they were not eager to have their young Dominican son go off to the United States, hoping to work among the Indians. Mazzuchelli gives an account of this in his *Memoirs,* in which he opens with a beautiful chapter explaining his vocation. "Absolute certainty," he writes, "of our vocation has never been granted through ordinary means, although we may be allowed to believe its existence, when time and results have, so to speak, proved the reality of one's election." He tells us, gently and with the utmost charity, how his family tried to hold him back, his father begging him to stay in Italy until his own eyes closed in death. Even to such an appeal he dared not respond in the requested way, so he left his native land never expecting to return.

He went straight upon arrival in America to Bishop Edward Fenwick of Cincinnati, a Dominican like himself, who sent him on to St. Rose's Priory in Kentucky, about 200 miles away. Having got to Louisville, he had to make the remaining thirty-eight miles on horseback. As this was his first riding lesson, and one over rough roads or none at all, he was so bruised and exhausted when he got to Bardstown, where Flaget was, that he had to keep to his bed for the next couple of days. Later he became hardened to this sort of life, an every-day part of missionary life on the frontier.

When he had completed his studies at St. Rose's and had been ordained, Fenwick appointed him "missionary apostolic" and sent him to Mackinac, where Marquette had been nearly a century and a half earlier. His work at this time was primarily with the Indians. Mazzuchelli quickly mastered the language of the Winnebago Indians and for them and the half-breeds prepared a prayer-book, which was printed in Detroit, and entitled *Ocangra Aramee Wawakakara.* Most of the converts the Jesuits had made in the seventeenth century had remained loyal to their religion, but, because since then they had seen a priest only at rare and irregular intervals, they were not too well instructed in the faith. Mazzuchelli did for these souls, scattered though they were, a solidly based work. During 1834 and part of the following year he was at Green Bay, visiting the Menominees and Winnebagos, but because whites had begun to stream in by the thousand, he was subsequently obliged to give much of his attention to them, without forgetting such Indians as he encountered. The church he built at Green Bay was the only one in the whole Territory of Wisconsin, nor was there any other priest there to give help to an utterly solitary man.

He had come out to do this work inspired by a sermon that Bishop Fenwick had preached at the Dominican house of studies in Rome. And it was all done with such disregard of himself that in his *Memoirs* he never mentions his own name; instead, he simply alludes to himself as "the priest" or "the missionary." As a historical document these *Memoirs* have high value. While they are written in a plain straightforward style, they contain a number of descriptive passages which show not only Mazzuchelli's power of close observation but much poetic feeling. The writer's selflessness is evident; furthermore, the reader cannot fail to see that he was a most engaging human being.

From the outset Mazzuchelli's methods were sometimes rather unusual. At Mackinac there was a Catholic whose conduct was reprehensible; in what way, we are not told. The local Protestants made him an example of what Catholicism was, for they would jeeringly tell one another: "It does not matter; the priest will always pardon him!" This made Father Mazzuchelli (or "Father Matthew Kelly," as he was often called) so indignant that he publicly reprimanded the man from the altar, and ordered that he stand at the church door with a rope around his neck, and in this way hear Mass every Sunday until Easter. It did much good to the man, and perhaps even more to his neighbors, for whose sake this public penance was devised. This sudden revival of methods prevalent during primitive times served the desired purpose among rough and simple people.

The Indians had their faults—perhaps only one very serious fault; keeping them away from "fire-water" was always a problem. However, those who were not Christians were sometimes polygamous, when they could afford to keep more than one wife. These plural wives were, not infrequently, sisters; one Indian explained to Mazzuchelli that this was "for the sake of keeping peace in the house," an explanation that amused him, while casting some light upon the disadvantages there might be in polygamy. He noticed that among the Indians old age was treated with such respect, that whites might in this instance take example from the savages. As for their priest, Mazzuchelli found there was not the slightest danger of his being molested; instead, the Indians were most kind and hospitable, giving him food freely and a corner of their cabins if he had nowhere else to sleep.

He was touched by the fervor of the Indian Catholics. At Sunday Vespers he managed to get them to chant the verses of the psalms alternately in Latin and their own language, adding: "The variety and pleasing effect of this new method of singing psalms aroused in the heart the sublime emotions suggestive of the grand Catholic unity and universality." He found the humility and simplicity they showed at confession very beautiful, for, when he encountered a tribe whose language he did not know, they had to tell their sins through an interpreter. This was for the pentinent an ordeal and took up much of the confessor's time, as everything had to be said twice. He remarks: "Whether the Catholic Indian is rigorously bound to make his private confession through an interpreter we shall not undertake to discuss here. The fact remains that he follows the safest path in his estimation, and in doing so, feels bound to all this, by submitting with unbounded simplicity and confidence to the Infinite Mercy." As for the devotion and frequency with which Holy Communion was received, a model was offered to all Christians. "Who," he asks, "at such a moment could refrain from giving thanks to God for this outpouring of divine light into the soul of a man whom the world would call rude and ignorant?" He was witnessing a wonderful transformation.

Mazzuchelli's own confessions were unavoidably rare because of his isolation. To find another priest he was obliged to make a long journey by canoe or on horseback, though now and then another priest visited him, as when Bishop Fenwick arrived with the future Bishop Baraga, a learned Austrian who produced dictionaries and grammars in several of the Indian tongues. Such a meeting was always a great occasion, and the sacrament of penance was always the first thing attended to, the priest who had heard the other priest's confession, immediately taking his turn as penitent.

So far from describing his life as hard, though often it must have been just that, one would think to read his *Memoirs* that he always found it delightful. His gun would bring him a meal of delicate wild fowl, which he would eat sitting upon the ground, with a strip of bark for a platter. Such a meal, he says, "was always more savory than the rich enjoy, who in abundance have no contentment, and know not what means the blessing of good appetite." But he found it a bit difficult to sleep upon the bare ground, and set about teaching himself to do this, by coming to it by degrees. He started this in his own room, lying upon two blankets on the floor; in the end he was able to rest quite comfortably, "thus making sure of a couch anywhere without expense."

Mass often had to be said in an improvised chapel of mats laid over poles. He commented: "The rich marbles of Italy were not needed for a pavement; that was perfectly supplied by the green grass in summer and by the hard frozen ground in the winter." When candles were to be had, their holders could be made out of birch bark. If there was no magnificence, this was more than made up for by the way the Indians assisted at Mass. Mazzuchelli could not recall an instance of the slightest irreverence; on the contrary, there was the most profound recollection. The baptized Indians would say from memory what few prayers they knew, the others looking on respectfully and in silence. As the doctrine of the resurrection of the dead made a powerful appeal to all Indians, Mazzuchelli often made this the theme of his sermons.

Like all the early missionaries among the Indians of the Great Plains, he was deeply impressed by the evidences of the piety of those who became Catholics. "As creatures endowed with reason and destined for the glory of the children of God, they were redeemed by God the Saviour." He did not fail to notice their faults, but he could make allowances. But he saw that for the permanent establishment of the faith among them a priest who knew their language should reside with each tribe, and that such a priest should erect a church, of however simple a sort, and provide a school, and foster agriculture as the main means of subsistence, instead of the hunting by which the Indians mainly lived. "In a total lack of all these things"—and the lack was almost total at that time—"the propagation of the faith would be a miracle in truth." Yet he had many consolations when he saw what fruit had come from his single-handed work.

It was, however, impossible—or at least inadvisable—for Mazzuchelli to be only a missionary to the Indians. The West was filling up too rapidly to permit this. We therefore find him devoting himself more and more after 1835 to the spiritual needs of the white settlers in the Territories of Iowa and Wisconsin and the State of Illinois. His centre of operations for a while was Dubuque, then only a little village, but rapidly growing because of the lead mines in the vicinity. In 1837 it was chosen as the see for a new diocese.

In 1838 the whole of Iowa had only 18,000 inhabitants, if we exclude the Indians. However, two years later the number had jumped to 43,000 and five years later to 70,000. Dubuque did not, as events turned out, ever become the immense city that was expected, but in Pierre Jean Loras, a Frenchman who since 1830 had been working in the diocese of Mobile, Alabama, it received its first bishop. Mazzuchelli himself could have obtained this bishopric, but there was nothing that he wanted less than to be a bishop, both because of his modesty and because he felt that his real work was of another kind.

There were good reasons for the creation of new dioceses, especially in the West, where everything pointed to rapid growth. For one thing, there was considerable difficulty of communication, even in districts that could be reached by the Ohio, the Mississippi and the Missouri rivers. Moreover, the presence of a bishop had the effect of attracting priests to his diocese. As Mazzuchelli put it: "Missionaries appeared in an instant; churches arose and overflowed with worshipers." Finally, having a bishop on hand ensured the protection of ecclesiastical property. Small and poor as all the churches in the West were, and not very valuable in monetary terms—except for a few in the dioceses of Louisville, St. Louis and Cincinnati—their erection had called for much hard work and sacrifice. If the provision that could be made for the support of the pioneer bishops was woefully meagre, the principle was cheerfully accepted: "What suffices for the priest suffices for the bishop." It was as in the first centuries, when the bishops worked without cathedrals or seminaries.

Loras, however, found a cathedral waiting for him when, after some delay he arrived at Dubuque—that of St. Raphael, named for the archangel who had befriended Tobias, and who is the patron of travelers. Of this, as was usually the case with the dozen or so churches built by Mazzuchelli, he himself was the architect. Generally, as not much money was available, and as those who contributed their services were not very skilled, it was a question of doing the best that such circumstances permitted. However, in the case of the cathedral at Dubuque, Mazzuchelli extended himself. His versatile skill may be observed in an altar he carved with his own hands and which is still to be seen.

While the building of the cathedral was going on, Mazzuchelli—except during frequent absences necessitated by projects elsewhere—lived under the sanctuary, in what was hardly more than an excavation for a cellar. It looked like a cave, but he made it serve as a house for himself. As for the churches he erected—the best of which, after St. Raphael's Cathedral, was that at Galena—there are an astonishing number.

For a time Mazzuchelli was chaplain of the Wisconsin legislature. Later he persuaded the senate of Iowa to hold its first sessions in the as yet undedicated church at Burlington. The rent that was paid for its use—$500—served to clear that church's indebtedness. It was very hard to resist this fascinating man. And as a preacher he had, in addition to the "presence" so valuable to an orator, what is even more valuable—a golden voice.

He had made Galena his chief station because it was situated on the road between Iowa and Wisconsin; he could therefore reach travelers easily there. His bedroom was merely a closet six feet long and five wide that opened out of the church. The quarters were extremely cramped and were stiflingly hot in summer and arctic cold in winter, but Mazzuchelli had the advantage of being only a few yards away from the altar. On the other side of the little church was his confessional. The body of the church he used as a study and the place where he received visitors.

Much of this time he had to go 500 miles or so down the Mississippi to St. Louis to make his confession. For these journeys he rarely incurred any expense, for the captains of the river boats—whether or not they were Catholics—knew that he employed all his time and labor for religious motives alone. Yet he had his moments of depression. In one of these he wrote: "One who is not of ignoble birth, and who knows that his training and ecclesiastical career deserve consideration, is strongly tempted on such occasions to consider it too great a humiliation." Again he says of himself, but using the third person: "His human pride, he confesses, did, now and then, rebel against daily dependence on the charity of others; but his spirit of evangelical poverty always won the vistory." We can only think all the better of this man that he does so frankly admit his temptations, but so far from having yielded to them he was able to say: "There is no doubt that the Christian religion was propagated primarily in the midst of poverty, and was born as it were in the cabins of the poor."

Mazzuchelli also started a college at Sinsinawa, serving as its president and chief professor. Though it had to be closed in 1866, two years after his death, Dominican Sisters took over the institution and have greatly multiplied, extending their work into many states of the West, especially California. Therefore, not even that project of the boundlessly resourceful Fr. Mazzuchelli can be said to have failed, but merely to have taken a somewhat different form because his untimely death left no other priest who could adequately replace him.

The last section of the *Memoirs* is quite impersonal, as it gives a brief but excellent account of the condition of the Catholic Church in the United States at that time. But it contains one sentence which may be partly accounted for by the state of his health while he was writing; ominously he says: "One in whose heart burns the flame of pure love for Truth, and who understands the position of our holy religion in America cannot but tremble for its future." When he said that Mazzuchelli was himself not at all well, and he was witnessing the eruption of antagonism and even mob violence towards Catholics. That moment of discouragement made this usually buoyant man for a moment a gloomy and therefore a false prophet. The difficulties that at the time seemed so threatening were in due course overcome. As Archbishop Ireland said in the introduction he wrote to the *Memoirs* when they were published in 1915: "A foreigner by birth, he was an American to the tip of his finger." It was as an American that he grieved over the country he loved.

Continuous hard work, with never a vacation, brought on a severe illness in 1843. From this he recovered, but friends managed to persuade him to take a long rest in Italy. It was at that time that he composed his *Memoirs*. As Archbishop Ireland says: "An exile, who never expected to see Italy again, he often stirred his fervor by contemplating [in thought] the stately temples of Milan and Rome, and . . . the splendors of the ceremonies there symbolical of the sublime grandeur of the Christian faith." It had to be so in the cabins that served as churches at Macinac and Green Bay, or the shacks in the lead-miners' camps at Galena and Dubuque. But there, and especially among the Indians, this great missionary saw evidences of a humble and tender devotion, and must have thrilled at the reflection that it was he who had planted the seed.

XV: Isaac Hecker

(1819–1888)

It would seem to be misleading to say that the most striking incident in the life of Isaac Hecker occurred three years after his death, for even apart from this, Fr. Hecker would still be one of the most interesting of American Catholics. In 1891 his friend and associate among the Paulists, Walter Elliott, published his life, a very able biography that one never would suppose to prove the occasion of any storm. Nor did it, when it was published in the United States, under the Imprimatur of Archbishop Corrigan of New York.

The trouble was caused by an inaccurate translation of the book into French, and the way that that translation was unjustifiably used—mainly because meanings were read into it which were not there, but were drawn out of it by a small group of somewhat "advanced" French priests to substantiate their own ideas, ideas that another more conservative group rightly reprehended. It was this misunderstanding on the part of both sides in the ensuing acrimonious controversy that impelled Pope Leo XIII to issue early in 1899 his Apostolic Letter, *Testem Benevolentiae.*

Both sides had used the term "Americanism," but the Pope in his condemnation was careful to term this "a false Americanism," and the propositions he listed were, in fact, heretical, or had a heretical tendency. To American Catholics this came as a great shock, as such ideas were quite unknown among them. When they assured Pope Leo that such was the case, what seemed at first a hurricane quickly died down. Nevertheless, ammunition was provided for anti-Catholic controversialists—as is true even in our own time in the case of men like Paul Blanshard, who, without bothering to indicate just what were the specific propositions that Leo XIII listed, find it suits them to say (ignoring the key word "false") that Americanism as such was condemned.

But the life and work of that very remarkable man Fr. Hecker, the innocent cause of the ancient turmoil, are more to our purpose. His grandfather was a German immigrant, a gentle sceptic with a sense of humor. Quite unconscious of the fact that the sixteenth-century Bavarian mathematician Nicholas Katzer had made almost exactly the same reply when King Henry VIII had asked him why he had not learned to speak English better after thirty years in England, old Hecker said, his eyes twinkling, when he was questioned: "How much English *can* anybody learn in forty years?" In his case, however, in the baker's shop he set up, he did not have much occasion to talk English. Beginning in a small way, and being industrious and living frugally, he started a business which made Isaac Hecker's elder brothers prosperous and eventually rather well-to-do.

These brothers had a bakery on Rutgers Street in New York City, and a shop on Pearl Street, to which the eleven-year-old Isaac used to carry their bread every morning for sale. Hard work was part of the family tradition, so little Hecker was not exempt from it. However, though like his brothers he had received little formal education, unlike them he showed intellectual interests very early, so that even when he was at the kneading trough he had—of all things in the world!—a volume of Kant propped up in front of him. How much he managed to get out of that tough philosopher may be a question, but it must have been enough to whet his desire for more.

The first powerful personal influence exercised upon Hecker was that of Orestes Brownson, partly because of philosophical speculations that were fascinating, but perhaps even more, in the beginning, because young Hecker, like Brownson himself, was deeply interested in social ideas of a radical kind. The tall gaunt Vermonter (in those days Brownson had none of his later burliness) was close to being the youth's idol. Brownson was a forceful and lucid lecturer rather than an orator, but Isaac found his mind immensely stimulating, so that almost from the start of their acquaintance the middle-aged editor and the young baker became fast friends. It was with the Heckers that Brownson usually stayed when he had an engagement to speak in New York, and Brownson and Isaac —and his brothers as well, since they too were actively interested in social questions—would sit up far into the night in eager conversation.

It was in 1843 that Isaac Hecker, who was then twenty-four, joined the colony at Brook Farm upon Brownson's recommendation. There Hecker would be among very idealistic —if sometimes slightly daft—people, and he would also obtain some instruction from gifted teachers and thus help to make good the deficiencies in his education. Some of the colonists paid wholly or in part by doing some work on the farm, and Isaac undertook to be the community baker, paying four dollars a week in addition. This part-time job left him free for his books.

By this time Brownson was clearly headed towards the Catholic Church, and whenever he paid a visit to Brook Farm he and Hecker talked about nothing but religion, to the mingled amusement and distress of the farmers. Though in later life Hecker could smile good-naturedly at some of the odd features of the farm, saying that it contained some who were "consecrated cranks," the deep effect it had upon his character was all for the good.

From Brook Farm Hecker went for a short while to stay with Bronson Alcott at Fruitlands in Concord, where Alcott looked benign and talked philosophy while Mrs. Alcott and her daughters did the work. Fruitlands, says Fr. Elliott, was a caricature of Brook Farm, as Hecker soon discovered. At

Concord, too, Hecker was at the centre of the transcendentalist group, though he was never one of them. Emerson he thought too vague to be satisfactory, but he studied Latin at Concord under George Bradford, an excellent scholar, while lodging with Mrs. Thoreau—who made a ridiculously small charge for room and board—and became a great friend of her son Henry.

Back in New York with his family Isaac Hecker began using a mild form of asceticism which indicates something of Alcott's influence. One of the entries in his diary reads: "My diet is apples, potatoes, nuts and unleavened bread. No water —scarcely a mouthful a week." Meanwhile, he was investigating all the forms of Protestantism, and for a while was inclined to become an Episcopalian.

Though Hecker may be considered Brownson's disciple, he preceded him by a month or two into the Catholic Church, both men being received in 1844. He already felt that he had a wider apostolic vocation than the ordinary priesthood. This he thought to obtain among the Redemptorists, joining them with two other remarkable men, Clarence Walworth, who threw in his lot with him when the Paulists were founded, and James A. McMaster, who found that he had no vocation to the religious life but who, as a layman, distinguished himself as the editor of the *Freeman*.

The three Americans who went to the Redemptorist novitiate in Holland were something of a puzzle to the novice master, though all of them were most exemplary. The impulsive and demonstrative McMaster was the easiest to comprehend, but Walworth was regarded as a "study" and Hecker as a "curiosity." But of course all Englishmen—and for ordinary purposes Americans are lumped with them—are regarded by continentals as slightly insane. Actually, there was nothing at all odd about Hecker; he was only of an unfamiliar type.

After they had completed their course of studies in Holland

and England, Hecker and Walworth returned to New York where, at the Redemptorist monastery on Third Street, they found Augustine F. Hewit, another convert from Protestantism, who was to become one of the original group of Paulists. Of these three, Walworth and Hewit were orators, Hecker a persuader, as such showing himself to be the most effective speaker of their group in later years. But to learn how to speak well in public called, on Hecker's part, for a lot of hard work, extending even to the modulation of his voice. In his work of persuasion, he was to a considerable extent under the guidance of Brownson, both men confidently counting upon bringing in a great many converts, especially from transcendentalist circles.

Yet there were marked differences between the two men. Where Brownson was primarily an intellectual, of a severely logical kind, Hecker was only secondarily an intellectual; primarily he was a mystic, a mystic of a very warm-hearted variety. The result was that Brownson, who had always been perhaps too much of a logician, and who became still more so because of Bishop Fitzpatrick's insistence that he use the scholastic method, now used logic to the virtual exclusion of everything else, except of a humor calculated to take the skin off the back of anyone who ventured to argue with him. He therefore only succeeded in alienating the somewhat fuzzy-minded friends whom he had hoped to win. Later in life he was to declare that logic—his kind of logic—was the very worst of all methods; but by then it was too late for him to change.

Hecker saw this; on June 29, 1845, he wrote of Brownson in his diary: "He is so strong and intellectually active that all his energy is consumed in thought. He is an intellectual athlete. He thinks for a dozen men. He does not take time to realize in heart for himself. His mind is of a historical rather than a poetical mould . . . He will never be charged with holding two doctrines, one esoteric and the other exoteric . . . His love of right is supreme, and the thing he detests is bad logic . . . He defeats but will never convince an opponent . . . No one loves to break a lance with him, because he leaves such ungentlemanly gashes." Hecker was not at all like that, except that he was as devoted to truth as was Brownson, but he presented his case with a good temper and sympathy that were impossible to his belligerent friend.

Hecker and the group of converts around him were very effective in the making of other converts. In later life Hecker, in fact, became so popular as a lecturer that he actually had to ask Catholics to stay away so as to leave room for the non-Catholics who wished to hear him speak. The book he published in 1857, *Aspirations of Nature,* had as its thesis that Catholic doctrine is a satisfaction of the demands that reason makes, just as the book that preceded it, *Questions of the Soul,* laid its emphasis upon the satisfaction that Catholic doctrine gives the heart. Hecker's main idea in his apostolic work was to leave much to natural inclinations, confident that, when unvitiated, they would lead to the Church. In short, *"Anima naturaliter Christiana."*

To quote, however, from one of his last articles, written in 1887, he said: "It is proper to say a word of the natural virtues and their relation to the supernatural. It has been already intimated that the goodness of nature is often indistinguishable from the holiness of the supernatural life; and, indeed, as a rule impulses of the Holy Spirit first pour their floods into the channels of natural virtue, thus rendering them supernatural. These are mainly the cardinal virtues: Prudence, Justice, Fortitude, and Temperance. Practised in a state of nature, these place us in our true relations with our nature and God's providence in all created nature around us; these are the virtues which choice souls among the heathen practised. They are not enough." The last four words show that, much as he allowed to uncontaminated nature, he is only saying that grace builds upon nature; in no way did he belittle the importance of grace. He wrote later in the same article: "The practice of the four cardinal virtues . . . in the ordinary natural state gave to guileless men and women in every age a natural union with their Creator. Although we maintain that such natural union with God is not enough for man, yet we insist that the part the natural virtues play in man's sanctification be recognized." This may be rather too optimistic in the sense of assuming that we may take this as ordinarily true of human beings—and it did provide a handle later which captious critics used against Hecker; but in the sense intended it was quite orthodox. He was directing his remarks against the notion of the total depravity of man, as maintained by Calvinists, and was seeking to offer encouragement to those who imagined that the Church's doctrine itself was grimly repellent, yet who, had it not been for this misunderstanding, might have felt attracted towards Catholicism.

Hecker and his friends who were using this mode of approach found that many of their Redemptorist brethren were somewhat out of sympathy with them. James Roosevelt Bayley, then Bishop of Newark, wished to have Hecker and his friends establish a Redemptorist house in his diocese, but that was not in accord with the wishes of the main body of Redemptorists in America. Under the old constitution of the Congregation, any of its members was allowed direct access to the superior general in Rome about important questions, and though the general chapter of 1855 had abrogated that rule, the new constitution had not yet been promulgated in America. Such being the case, Hecker felt himself free to avail himself of the older constitution and therefore made a journey to Rome to present his views.

To his shocked astonishment, immediately upon his arrival he was expelled for insubordination by the Redemptorist General. Moreover, he was informed that the money he had spent for his steamboat fare was a violation of the vow of poverty. Yet, peremptory though the general was, he invited

Hecker to stay in the Redemptorist house while he was in Rome, but Hecker, so as to be able to act more freely, took lodgings elsewhere. He found friends among some of the cardinals, and Pope Pius IX himself came to the rescue. He treated Hecker as though he had not been expelled; instead, he dispensed him (and those of his group) from their vows and gave them permission to form themselves into a new congregation. It was in this way that the Paulists came into being.

About the great work that the Paulists did there is no need to write here. But one or two distinctive features of the Paulists need to be touched on. If they did not take vows, they were not different in this respect from some other congregations—for instance, the Oratorians and the Sulpicians. Vows were not undervalued, but it was considered that, for the special work that these congregations undertook, they could be more effective without them. Nor did Hecker intend to disparage spiritual direction when he wrote: "The director is not to take the place of the Holy Spirit in the soul, but to assist His growth in the soul as its primary and supreme guide. The primary worker of the soul's sanctification is the Holy Spirit acting interiorly; the work of the director is secondary and subordinate."

These views of Hecker were later somewhat misunderstood and even misrepresented. Probably even his argument—to some extent derived from Brownson—that "the form of government of the United States is preferable to Catholics above other forms" caused, when put in that bald way, some misgivings. For, though it is true that the federal Constitution is, for this country, the best guarantee of religious liberty for Catholics (as also for Americans of other religious beliefs), the Church, strictly speaking, is perfectly willing to co-operate with any form of government, so long as this is not antagonistic towards the dogmatic teaching of the Church or contrary to the moral law.

First, however, Hecker's achievements in the field of journalism should be touched on. He founded the *Catholic World*, a magazine which is still with us. The following year he organized the Catholic Publication Society and in 1870 the *Young Catholic*. If the most important of all of Hecker's projects in this field did not materialize, it was only because his health began to fail and he never recovered it. This was for a daily newspaper, and one that had already been operating was offered for sale at the relatively low price of $300,000. Archbishop McCloskey at once offered to subscribe a large amount towards this, and Hecker's brothers, now men of some substance, were willing to play their part. Unfortunately, everything had to be dropped because Hecker was unable to bear the strain of editorship.

While remaining nominally editor of the *Catholic World* until his death, he did little more than control its general policy, give advice about special points, and occasionally write an article for it. It was Father Hewit who did most of the active work. As for Hecker's own articles, as is also true of his books, he considered it sufficient to make his meaning clear, without paying much attention to graces of style. But that he had excellent literary judgment is evident from one fact alone. One of the early contributors to the *Catholic World* was a young woman named Agnes Repplier. She wrote short stories for him—rather mediocre short stories—but he persuaded her that her true gift was for the writing of essays, and, at his urging, she switched to the essay and in this form obtained wide fame.

There were some differences of opinion with Orestes Brownson, who was the most notable writer for the *Catholic World*, though these differences were mostly due to the fact that the touchy Brownson could not always see eye to eye with Father Hewit, though even against him Brownson directed not much more than a growl and now and then a roar. In any event, it did not mean much, as the leonine old doctor quickly forgot any passing annoyance. Between Brownson and Hecker himself there remained the most cordial affection. In 1876 Fr. Hecker wrote to Henry Brownson, as soon as he heard of his old friend's death: "I owe more perhaps to your father than to any other man in my early life. My friendship and sense of gratitude to him has never been affected by any event during the last forty years." Some biographical interpretations, not based on available archives or a knowledge of masculine psychology, have failed to understand that men can argue heatedly with one another and yet remain firm friends.

During Hecker's last years he suffered a good deal from depression, what he himself called "almost unceasing desolation of spirit." Yet he added that his sufferings had greatly purified him and that God had given him comfort in the end. We must remember that Hecker was a sick man for nearly twenty years and make due allowances for this fact. He came to make allowances for himself and wrote: "I am tranquil, at peace, and doing nothing except willingly bearing feebleness and inertia." For a man like Hecker, so many years of relative uselessness are very hard to endure.

Often during those years he was unable to say his office. Then he would have some passages of the Bible read to him; "Without the Book of Job," he said, "I would have broken down completely." When he began to sink in October, 1888, a quiet calm returned. On the night of his death, December 20, he regained consciousness and gave the summoned community his blessing in a feeble whisper, raising his hand to make the sign of the cross; then, sinking into unconsciousness again, he died within an hour.

Fr. Elliott records his faults, such as they were; the greatest seem to have been that he was too easily imposed on, "crediting unworthy men who prated to him of liberty and the Holy Spirit; or overfondness during his illness for playing in the lists of fancy at an apostolate denied him in the battle of active life; he repined at being forced to plan great battles in a sick room." If that is the worst that can be said of him, it showed that he was consumed by the zeal for God's house, that his pure and tender heart was that of a great man.

XVI: James Augustine Healy

(1830–1900)

Anybody who visits Georgetown University will notice, as soon as he comes to the entrance gates, the largest and most imposing of its buildings. He will be told that this bears the name of Healy to honor the loved memory of a one time President of the University. What he is much less likely to hear is that this Fr. Patrick Healy was a Negro and that he was born a slave. However, it is not this particular Healy who is the subject of this chapter, but one of his two brothers who became diocesan priests in Boston: one of them being created Bishop of Portland, Maine; the other, who was probably even more brilliant, failing to obtain a mitre only because of his early death.

In several other countries there are many Negroes who are Catholic priests, and also some bishops, but it must be remembered that in the United States colored Catholics do not, even today, constitute a very large body, and that there is a paucity of vocations among them. While noting that three of the Healys rose to distinction in the Church, racial prejudice in their case proving no bar to advancement, it must also be admitted that in this matter American Catholics have no reason to boast. James Augustine Healy became a bishop in northern New England, not in the southern states, and not until he had been dead for more than half a century was his biography written.

During the war of 1812 a young Irish soldier named Michael Morris Healy who was on garrison duty in Nova Scotia deserted and contrived to make his way to Georgia. There at

Macon he prospered and bought a slave or two to help him on his little farm; eventually, he came to own over forty. One of these slaves was a sixteen-year-old mulatto girl named Mary Eliza, whose surname may have been Clark. Even her place of birth is not certain: she came from San Domingo, according to some accounts; according to others, from Virginia. Her master took her as his concubine, for the law of Georgia treated a marriage between a white and a Negro as invalid. However, it seems likely that he took her abroad for a marriage ceremony—otherwise, the illegitimacy of her children would have been a barrier to the priesthood of her sons. Healy always treated her as his wife, even though in Georgia she had a different status. That he referred to her in his will merely as "my trusty woman" indicates no more than that he could not do otherwise except at the risk of making his will invalid.

The tall handsome mulatto lived very happily with Healy, to whom she bore ten children, all of whom were, of course, legally slaves. Though many a white father in the South sold his children by a slave woman, as this father could have done, Healy was much too decent a person to perpetrate such a cruelty. Instead, he did everything within his power to protect them and their mother. He could not give them their freedom except by means of a special act of the legislature—and this was very difficult to obtain; therefore they remained slaves, though their servile status worried him a good deal.

Michael Morris Healy was not very strict in his practice of religion. Macon did not have a Catholic church at the time he went there, so he could not attend Mass, and by the time a church was built he had got out of the habit of attending Catholic services, though he continued to regard himself as a Catholic. If his children were unbaptized, this may have been because he was unaware that, under the circumstances, he could have baptized them himself.

At home the Healy children learned to read and write, but

not much more than that. There were no schools in Georgia which would have accepted them. Therefore, when the time came for them to get beyond the elementary instruction received from their father and (perhaps) their mother, they were taken for further education to the North. Even there it was not easy to find a boarding school that would accept Negroes, but James was able to attend one conducted by Quakers in Flushing, Long Island, and then another in Burlington, New Jersey. There the Healy boys showed themselves to be students much above the average. And though in the North they were still liable to be sent back under the law regarding runaway slaves, as nobody except their owner (who was their father) could invoke this law, they were safe. But as it would have been extremely risky to have brought them home during vacations, the best that could be done was for their father to come up from time to time to visit them. As this was a very inconvenient arrangement, he planned to give up his former intention of building a fine mansion on his plantation, and to sell all his holdings, and settle with his entire family in one of the free states.

In due course, the Healy brothers entered Holy Cross College in Massachusetts, doing this at the instance of Bishop Fitzpatrick, the coadjutor of Fenwick of Boston. When James was enrolled there, two of his fellow students were sons of Orestes Brownson. His sister Martha was taken in by the Bolands, relatives of the bishop.

Like his brother Sherwood, two years his junior, James wished to join the Society of Jesus. But, as at that time the Jesuit novitiate was in Maryland, a slave state, that plan had to be abandoned. The same situation barred the Sulpician seminary at Baltimore, so he became a diocesan priest. James and Sherwood were obliged to make the first part of their studies at Montreal, James then going on to Paris and Sherwood to Rome. It was only the younger Patrick who, as a result of the Emancipation Proclamation, was able to do what his elder brothers could not—become a Jesuit.

It might be noted that James Healy, when graduating from Holy Cross, received his degree from Georgetown, with which Holy Cross was then affiliated. It might be noted also that he headed his class, though it contained a Brownson, and that his younger brother Sherwood came fourth on the list—a decisive proof that the Negro does not belong to an intellectually inferior race. In addition, the Healys distinguished themselves as debaters. Their gifts were fully recognized by everybody—even by students from the South—and they were thought of as very acceptable young men.

James Healy was slight and somewhat diminutive in build, with brown eyes and bushy hair; though his complexion was not very dark, he was unmistakably a Negro. He does not seem to have been at all sensitive about this, and neither attempted to conceal or parade the fact. Instead, with easy aplomb, he brushed off any boor who tried, as happened a few times later on, to reproach him. His poise was remarkable.

It is not necessary to say much about the life of James and Sherwood as priests in Boston, except to point out that both became prominent in the diocese. Yet the Irish, who already constituted the most numerous body of Catholics there, were not as a rule very favorably inclined towards Negroes, largely because of their disgust with abolitionists, many of whom were religious bigots. The Healys got on rapidly, not primarily because they were protegés of the Bishop—Fitzpatrick had succeeded Fenwick in 1846—but because their talents were too obvious to pass unrecognized. As preachers, both Healys showed themselves to be much above the average, and those who belonged to an eloquent race appreciated eloquence in their pastors.

It might have helped, to some extent, that when Michael Healy died suddenly in 1850, his children were left rather well provided for. The hire of his slaves brought in about

$1,500 a year, and when they were sold to settle his estate, the sum they fetched was almost $35,000, to which must be added the value of his house and plantation. This meant that the Healy children had some private means. The main factor that operated, however, was their brilliance which, added to their piety, secured their position.

Even so, there was a time when, pending the settlement of his father's estate, James wondered if it might not be his duty to leave the seminary at Montreal, in order to work for the support of the younger members of the family. Only relative financial ease enabled him to decide to continue his studies for the priesthood under the Sulpicians at Paris.

After his ordination in 1854 Bishop Fitzpatrick appointed him pastor of one of the largest churches in Boston, and when John Joseph Williams succeeded Fitzpatrick in 1866, he made him his secretary and chancellor of the diocese, a very important position. He once was even credited with working a miracle when a great fire came towards his church, devouring everything in its path. It was then that Father Healy came out, prayer book in hand, before the onsweeping flames; and there he stood quietly praying, until, with a sudden change of the wind, the course of the fire was changed. Miracle or not, the incident became legendary. At least the diminutive Negro priest had proved his imperturbable courage as well as his faith, in the face of a fire which destroyed nearly 800 buildings in a sixty-five acre area.

Sherwood Healy was decidedly more negroid in features than James, though both showed their race clearly. Sherwood had come back from Rome holding doctorates in divinity and canon law. The two brothers became cordial rivals, and though James obtained the rectorship of the cathedral, Sherwood obtained a still larger church, and was thought to be marked out for a still higher position. It may be that James had a slight advantage with Bishop Fitzpatrick, for we hear of them cementing their friendship through music, the bishop sitting at the piano, while James sang plantation songs to his accompaniment. In almost every walk of life promotion all too often is due to personal backing. But this can hardly be said to be the case here, for Sherwood went ahead as fast as his brother, both of them being seen to be very exceptional men. The same was true of their Jesuit brother Patrick in his career at Georgetown.

James Healy had often been spoken of as a possible occupant of the see of Portland, Maine. When Bishop Bacon died in 1874, he became so in fact, although his appointment did not come until the following summer. His brother Sherwood also was mentioned as one who might succeed to the see of Hartford, Connecticut, but he did not live long enough to be offered the mitre.

When James Augustine Healy was appointed in 1875 as Bishop of Portland, a diocese over which he was to preside until his death twenty-five years later, there was a certain amount of grumbling about him as a Negro. Every once in a while he encountered reproaches, but most of these he was able to meet with the utmost tact and good humor. However, two situations were particularly distressing. Once, before he became bishop, he was barred from teaching catechism in a summer parish, and questions were raised about his legitimacy. More serious was a lawsuit over church funds and chancery records carried to the highest papal court by a priest whom Healy had been forced to discharge from office because of shady financial dealings and, later, of forgery. Though the bishop was completely cleared, the case left a lasting scar.

His greatest concern in the diocese of Portland was for the poor. He himself went out regularly to administer the last sacraments to the poor, or to anyone who was dying as a result of a street brawl, at the time a frequent occurrence. And in the parish school, which he named after his benefactor Winifred Kavanagh, a sister of Maine's only Catholic governor, he had his own way of discovering which of the children attending there belonged to needy families. Then he would appear at the house, bearing food and clothes; and as this was at a period when few working people earned more than nine dollars a week, and when even a policeman's job was refused to a Catholic, the bishop made himself a one-man agency for the relief of those in distress.

When he learned that his French-Canadians often had much more expensive funerals than the family could afford, he strictly limited the display that might be made, and insisted that the emphasis be laid upon the spiritual needs of the departed soul instead of a lavish expenditure that was flattering only to the bereaved.

Because he knew how general poverty was among his people, the bishop refused all invitations to dinner except in the houses of the few well-to-do families; he did not wish to embarrass hosts who, because he was to be a guest, would spend money they badly needed for other purposes upon his entertainment. Even his charities were bestowed by stealth; he often went to the kitchen door with his alms.

The Sisters of Mercy had been brought to Maine by Bishop Bacon in 1858, but it was under his successor that they really flourished. They came to staff most of his parochial schools, as well as several academies and a junior college for girls. When their American foundress, Mother Mary Warde, whose headquarters were in Manchester, New Hampshire (which was then part of his diocese), had her jubilee, Bishop Healy brought two archbishops and four other bishops and over fifty priests to honor the occasion. At the banquet it was the bishop himself who served Mother Warde and when at last, late in the afternoon, he found time to get a bite to eat, he contented himself with the leftovers at a corner of one of the tables in the refectory.

At the age of seventy he suddenly died. It was not from the pneumonia or tuberculosis with which most of his life he had been threatened, but a heart attack. After a sleepless night, during which the doctors shifted from their first conclusion that it was no more than acute indigestion, his nurse told him that he would have to take a long rest. In reply he answered: "Yes, and I am finally going to get one." By midday he had another seizure, and his curates were summoned to his bedside. Within a short while the life of America's only Negro Catholic bishop came to an end.

XVII: James Cardinal Gibbons

(1834–1921)

It has sometimes been said of James Gibbons, probably the most widely loved and influential American prelate, that his success was due not so much to what he did as to what he did not do—in other words, to his avoidance of mistakes. If so, that indicates marvellous discretion, for he repeatedly found himself in a situation in which it would have been easy for him to have blundered badly, yet those blunders he did not make. However, fully crediting him with wonderful discretion, he must also be credited with positive as well as negative virtues, for bold actions, that might have resulted in disaster, and not merely with the prudence which so often is the name with which timid caution plumes itself.

Up to the time of World War I, especially towards the end of the nineteenth century, the leadership of the "liberal" party in the American hierarchy was in the hands of Archbishop Ireland of St. Paul rather than of the Cardinal, though Gibbons as its most prominent member was the chief target of the conservative group. He was able, in conjunction with Cardinal Manning in England, to prevent Henry George's *Progress and Poverty* from being placed on the Index. He also managed—again with Manning's help—to get the Holy See to reverse its position regarding the Knight of Labor, the forerunners of the American Federation of Labor. Yet in each of these instances he met powerful opposition, and a set-back would have been very damaging.

Gibbons, and the Irish bishops of the conservative party also tangled with the dangerous situation described as

"Cahensleyism," a demand that, in dioceses in which German-speaking Catholics predominated, only German bishops should rule and German be virtually the official language. Not only Cardinal Gibbons, but also the majority of the bishops in the United States, perceived that if such special privileges were granted by the Holy See, and foreign enclaves be permitted in America, much force would be given to the prevalent idea that Catholicism was an exotic and foreign importation. It was touch-and-go for a while, however, though Gibbons had the support of a series of Presidents at Washington, who recognized that the only sound policy was that of assimilating immigrants, of whatever nationality, as soon as possible. While the demands of the more extreme "Germanizers" were in the end rejected by the Hold See, Germans in many cases held somewhat aloof, until the United States entered World War I. The fortunate defeat of "Cahensleyism" was achieved not through episcopal fulminations, but by a forbearing prudence.

The cardinal's affability and simplicity made him the friend even of the newsboys whom he encountered in his daily "constitutional." On these walks he was usually accompanied by one of the seminarians from Paca Street, and though primarily he was looking for a companion, he also gathered information about his future priests which was very useful to him. He may not have possessed the driving force of Archbishop Ireland, "the consecrated blizzard from St. Paul," but his affability and his prudence more than made up for any lack. And he showed that he could act with great courage when the situation called for it.

All the circumstances of James Gibbons's early life helped to prepare him for his later career. He was born on July 23, 1834, to Irish immigrants who had settled in Baltimore, and in its cathedral he was baptized. There were still people who had been alive when the Declaration of Independence was signed, and he grew up in its afterglow. The fact that his father returned to his native Ireland in 1837 because of failing health also was fortunate, as it gave James Gibbons an insight into the problems of the Irish immigrants, as did also the year of his return to the United States (1847), when the Nativists were concentrating their attacks mainly, if not solely, against the Irish newcomers. Though this time the family settled in New Orleans—where the Nativists were not strong—a few years later he went to Baltimore, a city where the "Plug-uglies," a branch of the Nativists, had a method all their own. It was in Baltimore that Gibbons entered the seminary and that he worked during the first four years of his priesthood, which had been conferred in 1861.

He was made a bishop when he was only thirty-four—working first as vicar-apostolic of North Carolina and then as Bishop of Richmond until in 1877 he became the coadjutor of Archbishop Bayley. As Bayley died before that year was out, Gibbons at the age of forty-three succeeded him as metropolitan. He was the youngest of all the bishops who attended the Vatican Council of 1869-70, and gained during this visit an insight into the evils which might flow from a politically directed union of Church and State, since he saw how a Catholic power such as Austro-Hungary could exercise undue pressure upon the Holy See.

In 1886 Archbishop Gibbons was created a cardinal; only McCloskey of New York had preceded him in the American church. It was under his presidency that the Third Plenary Council of Baltimore assembled, Gibbons also being empowered to act, but for that occasion only, as Apostolic Delegate. When McCloskey died the following year, Gibbons was the sole American Cardinal. Archibishops Farley of New York and William Henry O'Connell of Boston did not receive the red hat until the end of 1911.

There existed among some members of the American hierarchy an uneasiness regarding what was considered too liberal a trend—especially on the part of Archbishop Ireland, Bishop

Keane, Rector of The Catholic University, and Cardinal Gibbons himself. This had nothing to do with positive doctrine, about which all groups were perfectly orthodox, but with policy. Yet the Cardinal was always careful to weigh his words, and as he told his friend Archbishop Elder of Cincinnati: "I am always anxious about my public utterances. Speak out I must frequently. My position requires it. The public interests of the Church demand it. But I am always afraid of erring by excess or defect, and no one knows better than myself that my judgment is not equal to the demands upon it."

In 1892, in connection with the World's Columbian Exposition at Chicago, there was held a Parliament of Religions, in which representatives of all faiths took part. Gibbons was very dubious about the advisability of Catholic participation, but he yielded to others, though he wrote to Archbishop Ireland: "Any overt attempt on your or my part to suppress it would raise a hue and cry, and the worst possible motives would be attributed to us." He therefore suggested a noncommittal attitude and hoped that, if the parliament should meet, it would be for the last time. Quite definitely he was opposed to what some enthusiasts had suggested, that there be an international Parliament of Religions at a future date.

What was brewing may be found in what Archbishop Corrigan had written on April 22, 1892, to Father Hewit, who was editing the *Catholic World*, telling him: "When last in Rome, I was directed to repress certain Liberalizing tendencies" in the magazine. And it is likely that the uneasiness felt in Rome had some bearing upon the appointment early in 1893 of Archbishop Francis Satolli as Apostolic Delegate to the United States. Many of the American bishops were anything but enthusiastic about this, fearing that non-Catholic Americans would regard it as an infringement of the principle of the separation of Church and State. However, when it was made clear that the delegate was to be concerned only with ecclesiastical questions and would not have any diplomatic status, the fears of all reasonable people were removed.

As for the Chicago exposition, Gibbons received from the Pope a blessing upon the Parliament and Satolli went and spoke there. One of the things he said was: "Go forward, in one hand bearing the book of Christian truth and in the other the Constitution of the United States. Christian truth and American liberty will make you free, happy and prosperous. They will put you on the road to progress. May your steps ever persevere on that road."

The speech helped to clear the air further. Nevertheless, in the eyes of the American Protective Association (founded in 1887), the arrival of the Apostolic Delegate showed that the Pope was up to some new trick. An encyclical, which purported to come from Rome, was published in the A.P.A. paper, which said that on September 5, 1893, Catholics were to be absolved from their oath of loyalty to the United States, and that "on or about the feast of Ignatius Loyola, in the year of Our Lord 1893, it will be the duty of the faithful to exterminate all heretics found within the jurisdiction of the United States." When nothing happened on either date, the A.P.A. announced that the new St. Bartholomew's Day slaughter had been postponed; later, it offered the lame explanation that the forged encyclical had been planted on the A.P.A. by Jesuits. Quite ridiculous though all this was, the fact that an Apostolic Delegate to the United States had been appointed excited enough anti-Catholic bigotry to bring into the American Protective Association a large number of new members.

Satolli's arrival also had consequences of a different sort. One was that he ordered the reopening of the case of Dr. Edward McGlynn, who had been suspended from all priestly functions by Archbishop Corrigan, and then excommunicated for his refusal to go to Rome when summoned there. McGlynn, by taking the line that he was so certain of his orthodoxy that he was not going to answer the summons, had shown foolish truculence; he was now more amenable and at Satolli's request prepared a statement of his views, which the committee of professors at the Catholic University appointed to examine it found unobjectionable. He could have saved himself a great deal of trouble had he only presented himself in Rome.

The "heresy" reprehended by Corrigan—at the urging of Bishop McQuaid—was that McGlynn had advocated Henry George's single-tax theory, and had publicly advocated George's election as mayor of New York. Few single-taxers can be found today, but there were a good many at that time, and in Corrigan's view they were scarcely to be distinguished from Communists. The *Rerum Novarum* of 1891 reaffirmed the principle of private property, and this was taken by those opposed to George to be a condemnation of his ideas. It would have been precisely that had the single tax been a negation of the right to private property, but George had satisfied Cardinals Manning and Gibbons that it was nothing of the kind. Now, when McGlynn drew up his version of the meaning of the single tax, it was accepted, and Corrigan was ordered by the Apostolic Delegate to reinstate him. This of course was done, yet, as Corrigan could not put him back as pastor of St. Stephen's, the largest church in New York City, he was appointed to Newburgh, where he would draw little attention.

Unfortunately, much harm had been caused. The majority of the parishioners of St. Stephen's had been strong partisans of their ejected pastor, and a number of them left the Catholic Church over the way McGlynn had been treated. To this day some of their descendants carry on the old quarrel, blaming the Holy See instead of placing the blame on the protagonists, Corrigan and McGlynn. Yet the Archbishop had done good work in other directions. He had built the seminary at Dunwoodie and had helped save the North American College at Rome from confiscation by the Italian government, largely through the negotiations of President McArthur and his Secretary of State.

The so-called "liberals" could point to other victories they won, in the field of education. Archbishop Ireland had allowed parochial schools at Stillwater and Faribault, which were within his diocese of St. Paul, to be integrated with the public-school system. As most of the inhabitants were Catholic, Sisters wearing their habits, were the teachers; but such Protestant children as attended were not obliged to attend religious instructions. About this connection of the schools with those of the state, complaints were made to the Holy See, which, however, decided that the arrangement could be "tolerated." But on September 17, 1892, Satolli read to the assembled archbishops in New York a long statement which prohibited any priest or bishop from excluding from the sacraments any parents who sent their children to a public school. Article 7 of this statement ran: "The Catholic Church, in general, and especially the Holy See, far from condemning or treating with indifference the public schools, desires rather that, by the joint action of civil and ecclesiastical authorities, there should be public schools in every state, according as the circumstances of the people require, for the cultivation of the useful arts and natural sciences; but the Church shrinks from those features of public schools which are opposed to the truths of Christianity and morality, and since, in the best interests of society itself, these objectionable features are removable, therefore not only the bishops but the citizens at large should labor to remove them, in virtue of their own right and in the cause of morality." This was not a new declaration of policy, but a clarification of the Church's position.

McQuaid naturally was furious and on December 13th of

the same year wrote to Corrigan: "We are all in a nice pickle, thanks to Leo XIII and his delegate . . . It is only a question of time, when present Roman Legislation, having wrought incalculable mischief, that we, school-children of the hierarchy, will again receive a lesson in our Catechism from another Italian sent out to enlighten us." Archbishop Ireland, backed by Cardinal Gibbons, had clearly won the round. Yet neither regarded the school arrangements of the St. Paul diocese—which were not unlike those that had been used in up-state New York, and which are still used here and there—as more than making the best of matters as they existed.

A far more serious issue then arose. The Catholic Church condemns all secret societies and excommunicates any Catholic who joins one. Cardinal Taschereau of Quebec condemned the Knights of Labor as a secret society, and was at first supported by the Holy See. But Cardinal Gibbons, not satisfied that this was just, asked the head of the Knights (their Master Workman) to see him, becoming completely convinced as a result that they did not constitute a secret society at all. He therefore undertook to go to Rome to try and get the condemnation withdrawn, and succeeded in doing so. But as he said years later to A. S. Will, whom he had selected to write his biography: "Ah, what a struggle it was on both sides of the water! I had so many difficulties that I wonder I got through them. Bishops are so hard to persuade!"

Peace came at last to the factions. As for Gibbons, who survived Ireland by three years, and McQuaid by twelve, his last years were serene but not very eventful. He was eighty-seven when he died, greatly honored by Americans, whatever their religion. He had been a bishop for fifty-three years, Archbishop of Baltimore for forty-four, and a cardinal for thirty-five.

The Catholic Church in America has produced several men who may have been abler than James Gibbons, and perhaps a few greater men, but there has never been one with just his combination of qualities—prudence, when it was called for, shrewdness of judgment, affability and benignity, but also resolute courage. He was for all Americans the outstanding Catholic of the age in which he lived. And his book, *Faith of our Fathers,* published in 1877, the year in which he became Archbishop of Baltimore, has been the most phenomenal best-seller ever written by an American Catholic. It is still a standard work in the field.

XVIII: Francesca Cabrini

(1850–1917)

Francesca Cabrini was the first citizen of the United States to be canonized. The general rule is that a cause for beatification is not even to be opened until fifty years after a candidate's death. But within eleven years Mother Cabrini's cause was introduced; ten years later, the title of *Blessed* was conferred by Pope Pius XI, and after seven years more the present Pope elevated her to the full rank of sainthood.

Mother Cabrini, though she became naturalized, remained Italian in feeling to the very marrow of her bones, despite the fact that her main work was done here. In the land of hustle and bustle and big business this frail woman, who until her arrival here in 1899 had little experience in practical affairs, showed over and over again an astonishing business acumen. As for the hustle and bustle, she was so constantly on the move—going not only all over the United States but to Central and South America, and to France, Spain and England—that sometimes it is a little hard to keep sight of her because of the dust, so to speak, that her heels kicked up.

Ever since she had been a little girl Francesca dreamed of going to some foreign country as a missionary; it was because of this that later she added Xavier to her name. Of course, when so small, she had no idea how her ambition could be carried out. Indeed, as a young woman she twice applied for admission to religious orders, in one case to an order in which she would have had to renounce her dream, but a second time to another which had a mission in China, in the hope that she might be sent there. In both instances she was refused, ostensibly on the ground of her poor health, though actually (as she discovered later) because Monsignor Seratti, the provost of the little town of Codogno, wished to use her in a project of his own.

Francesca Cabrini was born on July 15, 1850, at Lodi. Her family was of peasant stock, and her parents and their twelve children were all very pious. Francesca's mother was fifty-two when this last child was born. Her upbringing fell largely into the hands of Rose, the eldest of the Cabrini daughters, who was, quite unnecessarily, a martinet. Yet Francesca said in later life that the absolute obedience Rose demanded had done much for her.

Even before Francesca's confirmation at the age of seven, the neighbors used to speak of the fair-haired child as the "little saint." After her confirmation she became even more pious, and her ambition to be a missionary seems to date from then, though she does not appear to have spoken of it until she was about thirteen, only to have the sharp-tongued Rose jeer at her. Her favorite game was making little paper boats and sailing them on the river, filled with violets. The violets typified the missionary Sisters whom she intended to send all over the world.

When Francesca was nine she saw the white-uniformed Austrian soldiers march through the town, and march out again that summer. Three years after that she saw Garibaldi when he visited Lodi. Her father's cousin was the Agostino Depretis who was to become prime minister of a united Italy. He proved to be of considerable help to her several times, times when she badly needed help.

At thirteen she went to a convent school at Arluno, staying there five years. After this she attended a normal school, for, as both her father and her mother were dead by now, it was necessary that she earn her living as a teacher. Though not exactly a brilliant scholar, she had a keen intelligence. She says she learned Latin and French "in a practical way"—that is, going no further than to obtain what would serve her purpose. She also was good at mathematics, which proved more useful to her, in view of the business deals she had to handle after coming to the United States.

After she had taught school for a short while, Monsignor Serrati persuaded her to go to a badly managed orphanage at Codogno to straighten out its affairs. It was under the charge of a woman named Antonia Tondini, who had put up the money to found it, but who soon got herself into financial muddles. Things came to such a pass that the Bishop of Lodi induced her, a friend, Teresa Calza, and their cook, Giuseppa Alberici, to adopt a semi-religious habit, in the hope that this would be conducive to a more regular life. They constituted merely a small diocesan community and were known as the Sisters of Nazareth.

As no very noticeable improvement resulted, Monsignor Serrati tried another plan. If only Francesca would stay there for a couple of weeks, he said, he was sure that she would bring order out of chaos. When the two weeks were up, he begged her to stay on, and Francesca felt that she could not abandon the hapless orphans. Instead, together with five of the girls there, she was invested with the habit on October 15, 1874.

Though Francesca was now, at least technically, a novice in a sisterhood, the monsignor did not let her take her vows until three years later. As soon as Francesca had made her profession, the monsignor told her to sit in the sanctuary and receive the vows of the five girls, who had entered at the same time she did. Francesca complied, but with a quaking heart, for she had already fully discovered how impossible it was to deal with a shouting and screaming Antonia Tondini. In 1880, after considerable recrimination, as well as insubordination, the latter brought suit for the money which she had put into founding the orphanage, and the money and rambling house were returned to her. The bishop, however, thereupon also had to dissolve the community as such.

This meant that Francesca and seven young Sisters (including the former cook of the orphanage) had to find another home. Monsignor Serrati bought them one for 10,000 lire, which came out of his own pocket and that of the bishop. It was an old Franciscan friary which had remained deserted since Napoleon had closed it. There was nothing left there except a few mechanics' shops on the ground floor. But knowing that the price would be raised if the owners knew who were the purchasers, the monsignor used an architect friend as the ostensible buyer, and he gave it out that the place was to be used as a storage for lime. Francesca laughed when she heard about this and commented: "Yes, that's quite true; with our lime we are going to put up strong spiritual buildings all over the world." The missionary ambitions of her girlhood, which had been in abeyance during the six years she had spent in the orphanage, and which, even there, had not been completely abandoned, now came surging back as strong as ever.

This missionary activity could not so much as begin until Francesca had consolidated her new community, chosen a name for it—the one finally decided upon was that of the Missionaries of the Sacred Heart—and had drawn up a rule. Moreover, she had to recover from the strain of living in the same house as the strident termagent Tondini, and to obtain more recruits for the work she intended to do. The former Franciscan friary had to be enlarged, and, as money for this was lacking, the little group that now occupied it tried their hands at building. As might have been foreseen, a wall put up by completely inexperienced female bricklayers tumbled down. In later years, however, Francesca personally supervised the construction of several Sisters' houses.

Their habit was the same as the one they had worn in the orphanage, except for one or two slight alterations. But after they went to the United States a veil—such as would not interfere with their work—was added, and this still is the dress of the Missionary Sisters of the Sacred Heart.

Though hers was at the start only a diocesan institute, Francesca did not wish that it should remain merely that. Her vision was world-wide. After opening new convents near Cremona and at Milan, she descended upon Rome to get papal approval of her community and its rule, and, she hoped, permission to open a house there. Monsignor Serrati warned her that Rome was already overstocked with convents, and that she would almost certainly not obtain sanction for further expansion.

But it was not easy to daunt Mother Cabrini. She went to see Cardinal Lucido Maria Parrochi. He received her most affably, but said much the same thing that Monsignor Serrati had already told her, that she had better return to Codogno. However, like so many people, he yielded to her charm and forthrightness, and ended by placing her in charge of two convents in Rome instead of the one she had asked for. And Pope Leo XIII, when at last Francesca saw him, was also deeply impressed.

But when she told him of her ambition to go to China, he thought a moment and then said: "No, not to the East but to the West, my daughter." He said he wished to obtain a community of Sisters to work among the neglected Italian immigrants in the United States.

The Third Plenary Council of Baltimore, when it met in 1884, had discussed this very problem, but had found no solution beyond inviting Don Bosco to send some priests across the Atlantic, something which he had to tell them he found it impossible to do for at least two years. Then Bishop Scalabrini of Piacenza took the matter up, forming the Congregation of St. Charles Borromeo for this purpose. Even so, he could send only a few, and in the whole of the United States at that time there were only a dozen or so Italian priests. The peak of Italian immigration was still far distant, but even then, in New York City alone, where the Scalabriniani Fathers were at work, there were 50,000 of their countrymen. And not one in forty of them went to Mass.

This was not always the fault of the immigrants, because, except for the handful of Scalabriniani and a few men who had been at the American College at Rome, there were no priests who could hear confessions in Italian. Moreover, the Irish and German clergy could not always understand the poverty of church collections, nor could the Italians understand their demands, as in their own country there were no collections. Further, some of the immigrants who had preceded them to our shores, just because they had been kicked around in their time, now were disposed to administer a few kicks to the Italians. Not many skilled artisans came to America, and as even the demand for waiters and barbers was limited, the majority could obtain no work except that of the roughest, hardest, most dangerous and least well paid sort. To make matters worse, they were preyed upon by their own *padrones,* who demanded a fee for every service, however slight, yet without whose aid they did not find it easy to get work.

Though commissioned to go to the United States by the Pope himself, Mother Cabrini prudently asked Bishop Scalabrini to sound out Archbishop Corrigan as to whether he would welcome them. Corrigan answered cordially, and the Contessa Cesnola, wife of an expert at the Metropolitan Museum of Art, wrote to say that she had a house ready for their occupancy as an orphanage on East 59th Street. Unfortunately, she had neglected to tell the Archbishop of her plans, and he expressed strong objection that they were not planning to settle in "Little Italy" on the lower East Side. After many misunderstandings after their arrival, they were lodged in an orphanage of the Sisters of Charity at the corner of Madison Avenue and 51st Street.

After a very short time, the archbishop was quite won over and charmed by the valiant little woman, and became her firm friend. She, for her part, also saw that the archbishop had been right in his objection to the 59th Street location, for nearly all their work was on Mott and Mulberry Streets, or in teaching a school in the gallery of the Scalabriniani church on Roosevelt Street. While Francesca was with the archbishop on one of his visitations he pointed across the Hudson to Manresa, which the Jesuits were giving up as their novitiate, as they were preparing to move to Poughkeepsie. "Now there," said Corrigan, "is where you ought to be."

This happened during her second visit to America, when she returned with seven more Sisters, having taken back two American girls to make their novitiate at Codogno. Mother Cabrini now learned that Manresa—or West Park, as she renamed it—could be bought for a song. And when she went to see the house, which was indeed commodious and in beautiful and healthful surroundings, she knew at once that this was the very place she had seen in one of her dreams. She added that she would be buried there—a correct prophecy, though now her remains have been transferred to the chapel of the fine high school that has been built on what is now called Cabrini Avenue in upper New York City.

Just how Francesca raised the money to buy the house offered her is a mystery, for though the Jesuits asked a very low purchase price, it was still large enough to stagger her. Presumably, the archbishop himself may have made a sizable contribution, and friends in Italy did what they could, but it was always found that, when in pressing need for funds, Mother Cabrini could draw upon her "heavenly bank" by saying to one of the Sisters: "Just open that drawer on the left"—and sure enough the exact sum needed was there.

Soon after this, in the middle of September, 1891, Francesca was able to take fourteen Sisters to Nicaragua, where a wealthy lady had given them a large building suitable for an academy. On every occasion, with but one exception, Francesca opened a new foundation in person. She stayed in Nicaragua until the academy was prospering; then, at the beginning of March, 1892, she sailed for New Orleans, on her way across the isthmus projecting a mission for the Indians she encountered. This design she was never able to carry out, but that it occurred to her shows how insatiable was her zeal. Subsequently, even the Nicaragua school had to be given up, as the Sisters there were forcibly ejected as a result of a revolution. A later government had to apologize before she would consent to send Sisters to Nicaragua again.

She arrived in New Orleans a year after an outrage had occurred there. Eleven Italians accused of some crime had been acquitted at their trial. Nevertheless, a mob broke into the jail where some others were waiting to go before the judge, and hanged them on trees and lamp posts, along with those who had been acquitted. Mother Cabrini immediately decided that the Italians of New Orleans needed her help. At her summons several young Sisters traveled South, but could pay their fare only by getting tickets to whatever point they had money to pay for, and then getting off the train to beg some more. By these means they eventually reached New Orleans, where their first "convent" was a squalid apartment in the Negro section, from which they brought material and spiritual succor to the terrified Italians.

Back in New York, Mother Cabrini yielded to the persuasions of the Scalabriniani to take charge of a small hospital they had opened on East 109th Street, though hospital work had never been part of her plans. However, she soon found that she was expected to make herself responsible for the debts of the institution. She thereupon decided to withdraw and to found a hospital of her own on East 12th Street.

She did so with a capital of $250. But she was always fertile in resource: as Columbus Day was approaching, she decided to name her hospital after the discoverer of the New World, thereby obtaining the support of all Italians, even the anti-clerical ones. And every hospital she subsequently opened—in New York alone there are two, with another two in Chicago—was named for Columbus. She managed at all only because most of the food and medical supplies were donated, and the doctors gave their services free of charge. Also, the Italian consul arranged that any sick Italian sailor was to be received, the government at home bearing the expense. Many of the rest of the patients were accepted and treated without payment. Though Francesca did not live to see the Columbus Hospital now on East 19th Street in operation, she herself supervised every detail of the plans.

After an interlude in Italy, where she visited all the houses she had established—which now included a normal school and a hostel for working girls, as well as the orphanages with which she had commenced operations—she returned to the United States. From there she went on to Argentina, where she opened two new schools. She went there by way of Peru, crossing the Andes on mule-back, and on her return stopped at Sao Paulo to found yet another school.

Then she went to France, and she opened a boarding house for ladies near the Arc de Triomphe. This brought her into contact, through one of her boarders, with the Infanta Eulalie. As a result, she was invited to Spain. There the queen mother asked for two of the Sisters to live in the Escorial to act as governesses of the royal children. Though this offer was refused, Francesca did open a school for the aristocracy of Madrid, the queen mother ransacking the royal storehouses to obtain furniture, carpets and hangings.

Then came England, and Francesca was enchanted with the English people, saying that none she had ever met were so kind and courteous. Again a school was opened in one of the London suburbs, intended primarily for the Italian colony.

Upon her return to the United States there occurred what

was perhaps the most characteristic and amusing of her exploits. In Chicago, on the north shore, right on the lake, a hotel that had once been fashionable was for sale cheap. But when she told Archbishop Quigley that she had only a thousand dollars available, he had to tell her that was not going to get her very far. She therefore set out to collect among the Italians of the city, with Sister Xavier de Maria.

Enough was gathered to make a down payment, but Mother Cabrini suspected that it was planned to defraud her of a valuable strip on the edge of the block the hotel occupied. Therefore, with peasant canniness, she and Sister Xavier went out early one morning and with bits of string took the exact dimensions of the lot she had agreed to buy. At the closing of the deal she was able to confront the owners with the fact that their figures were incorrect, and so got all that she had bargained for.

Others attempted trickery of another sort upon Mother Cabrini. During her absence from Chicago contractors started so many expensive and unnecessary alterations, beginning to dismantle almost the whole interior of the hotel, that Mother Cabrini upon her return, just in the nick of time, fired the contractors, promising to expose them if they brought suit against her. Then she engaged new workmen, whose every operation she minutely scrutinized, thus saving many thousands of dollars. She had learned a lot since that time when the brick wall built by the Sisters themselves at Codogno had fallen down.

She paid little attention to the card-index side of the business, and, indeed, could never have said precisely how many Sisters were in her congregation, though each of them she knew well, and though every Sister felt herself the special object of loving solicitude. Her tasks had become very varied, for without forgetting the orphanages with which she began operations, she put most of her later emphasis upon schools and hospitals. Moreover, Sisters were sent to the mining camps of Colorado, where they would go deep down the mine shafts and miles along underground tunnels to find the Italian miners, who were overjoyed to hear their own language in the mouths of these smiling women. To Sing-Sing, as the prison chaplain could not speak much Italian, she also sent Sisters. The same was true at the jails in Chicago; there the Sisters more than once prepared the condemned for death, staying with them to the last moment before they were taken to the death chamber, even sometimes helping to draw their masks over their faces—and then emerging in a state of collapse.

At Denver Francesca established a hospital and another in California, though there it was rather a preventorium for children who were threatened with tuberculosis. It was during this time that she remained in this country for a long enough period to become naturalized. Without conflict with her pledge of allegiance to the country where most of her work was done, she remained inescapably Italian in feelings. Although she did not restrict herself to immigrants from the land of her birth, naturally she directed herself primarily to them; it was precisely for that that at Leo XIII's request she had come to the United States.

In 1910 she attempted to resign as superior general and to retire to a life wholly devoted to prayer. However, the other members of her congregation effectually prevented her from setting down her burden. They wrote to every house of their congregation, all of whom voted unanimously that she be retained. They then presented these votes to Cardinal Vives y Tuto, Prefect of the Congregation of Religious, and he joined their conspiracy. Then on Francesca's sixtieth birthday he summoned her and a delegation of her daughters and, jesting with grim humor, but smiling immediately afterwards, he said: "Mother Cabrini, though up to now you have governed your institute badly, I have decided to give you another chance: you are to remain superior general."

As a supreme act of obedience, she accepted the decision. But she replied with matching humor: "Well, I warn you that I shall be just as severe as in the past."

Renewed vigor came for a while to Francesca. But, though she made several new foundations, it became very evident that her health was failing. When she got back to Chicago for the last time, after opening a house in California, she seemed at death's door. Nevertheless, the astonishing woman rallied, and hope revived that she would be spared for a few more years, for she was only sixty-seven. A long rest at the Columbus Hospital on the North Shore would restore her. She did not remain in bed very long, but continued to potter around; a few days before Christmas she was busy filling bags for the children in a school taught by her Sisters and wrapping up a few presents for friends. One was for Archbishop Mundelein, not yet a cardinal. For each of the Sisters she also had a Christmas present—a new habit.

On December 22 she was sitting in her room at the hospital, waiting for one of the Sisters to bring her her lunch. Just then the waiting Sister heard Mother Cabrini's bell suddenly rung. Knowing this to be a signal of distress, she went in quickly, the lunch tray still in her hand, and found Mother Cabrini fallen back in her chair. The doctor and chaplain and the rest of the community were immediately summoned, but there was nothing that could be done, except for the priest to administer extreme unction. She recovered herself just enough to open her eyes and turn a last look on her daughters. Then peacefully she breathed her last.

XIX: Rose Hawthorne Lathrop

(1851–1928)

Rose Hawthorne Lathrop, the younger daughter of the great novelist, Nathaniel Hawthorne, was born in Lenox, Massachusetts, on May 20, 1851, "a child of spring, and spring never vanished from her nature," as her brother Julian wrote five years after her death. This matches what her father said of his wife, the charming and brilliant Sophia Peabody, "I have married the Spring! I am husband to the month of May!" In that respect Rose Hawthorne had much of her mother in her; looking more deeply at her, one may discern even more of her father.

When the children were still quite young, the Hawthornes moved from Lenox to Concord, to a house next door to that occupied by Bronson Alcott. And there they lived until Franklin Pierce, Hawthorne's great friend since their college days at Bowdoin, became President of the United States. Knowing that the author, though already famous in America, was having a rather hard struggle for existence, the President appointed him American consul at Liverpool.

This set Hawthorne firmly upon his financial feet; indeed, he was for the first and last time in his life almost affluent. While Hawthorne may not have found the office routine of his consulship much to his taste, he knew that he was extremely fortunate. He not only had his salary but (what has long since ceased) the right to pocket the fees charged for every ship that docked there. And as Liverpool in those days was the main port for ships that crossed the Atlantic he obtained a good deal of money from that source alone.

Though he did not regard his appointment as merely a sinecure, he could delegate many tasks to subordinates and find time for the keeping of a voluminous account of the English and of his travels in England which he called *Our Old Home*.

His keen eye took in more clearly than most Englishmen do the fact that England was once a Catholic country, for the evidences of that past were everywhere. After Buchanan's election as President, Hawthorne lost his consular position, but he had saved enough for a long stay in Italy. Out of that came *The Marble Faun,* and though as a New England Unitarian he was inclined to be critical about the number of apparently well-fed priests he saw on the streets of Rome, he was fascinated by the Catholic Church. Despite the attraction, he never showed the slightest desire to join it.

Rose, who was thirteen when her father died, had obtained at various private schools as good an education as most girls ever received in those days, and from America eventually went to Dresden in Germany to study art. For this, however, as for the music that she had earlier taken up, her talent was slight. Nor when she came to recognize this, and began to write, was she outstanding, though she wrote a good many short stories and poems, often placing them in leading magazines.

She was with her mother in London when the delightful Sophia died, and soon afterwards, when she was about twenty, she married the young writer George Parsons Lathrop. He was an energetic and versatile person, and was looked upon as an up-and-coming young man. But, conditions being what they were at the time for writers, he and Rose found it hard to make ends meet. George did become an assistant editor of the *Atlantic Monthly,* produced a rather unsatisfactory biography of his father-in-law in 1876, and supervised a new edition of Hawthorne's collected works.

George and Rose Lathrop became well enough off to buy back The Wayside, the Hawthornes' house at Concord which

Sophia had sold after her husband's death, and there he produced a couple of volumes of competent, if uninspired, verse, a travel book about Spain, and, after he and Rose became Catholics, a book about the Georgetown Visitation Convent in collaboration with her. Before he died he also wrote several not very successful plays and an opera to which Walter Damrosch wrote the music.

The death of the only child the Lathrops had—a son Francis, for whose sake they had bought The Wayside—was a severe blow. Therefore, they sold the house and, after living for a while in New York, bought a house in New London, Connecticut. Rose may have persuaded George to settle there to get him away from the too convivial friends he had made in the larger city. If so it did not work very well.

That George had started to drink too much, passing from that stage to alcoholism, one suspects was largely due to his disappointment with himself as a writer. For though the work that flowed from his pen could always be disposed of, he had hoped for greater things. He was still sanguine, but one senses in his unpublished letters a querulous note. His drinking was certainly not conducive to a happy marriage.

Possibly Rose herself was somewhat difficult at times. Unpublished letters reveal that there were several separations, followed by reconciliations. But the situation became worse, and in 1894 Rose was forced to ask the Bishop of Hartford to authorize her to leave a husband who had grown dangerously violent. He loved her to the end, and she loved him, but it had become impossible for them to live together any longer.

Apparently they did not meet again until George lay dying in April, 1898. He had struggled on bravely, but was broken up when Rose left him, producing for serialization a bit that somewhat forecasts today's "science fiction," but far more reminiscent of Bellamy's *Looking Backward,* and other odds and ends of writing, his chief source of income being a not too well paid job in connection with the management of Augustin Daly's theatre. Out of what he earned, which was not a great deal, he may have managed to send Rose a little money from time to time, and she may have been able to salvage something from the Hawthorne estate, which was not large, but she was, if not destitute, not at all well off.

Sixty years ago there were not many jobs open to women, other than as domestics. Rose tried to support herself by selling short stories and poems. Yet it was the tragedy of her married life that was to open the door to her real vocation. Hers is a striking instance of how a woman, brilliant yet baffled in everything she had attempted, stumbled, when nearing forty, into the one thing that she showed she could do supremely well.

She had been prepared for this by her conversion. But it also is possible to find in several passages of her father's *English Notebooks* something of the compassion that drove her to the succor of the afflicted. One of these must suffice: "We went," Nathaniel Hawthorne had written, after a visit to a workhouse, "into the ward where the children were kept; and on entering this, we saw . . . two or three very unlovely and unwholesome little imps, who were lazily playing together. One of them . . . immediately took the strangest fancy to me; it was a wretched, pale, half-torpid little thing, with a humor in its eyes, which the governor said was scurvy. I never saw (till a few moments afterwards) a child that I should feel less inclined to fondle. But this little, sickly, humor-eaten fright prowled around me, taking hold of my skirts, following at my heels; and at last held up its hands, smiled in my face, and standing directly before me, insisted on my taking it up! Not that it said a word (for I rather think the imp was underwitted and could not talk), but its face expressed such perfect confidence that it was going to be taken up and made much of, that it was impossible not to do it. It was as if God had promised the child this favor on my behalf (but I wish He had not!) that I must needs fulfill the contract. I held my undesirable burden a little while; and after setting the child down, it still followed me, just as if (God save us!) it were a child of my own. It was a foundling; yet out of all human kind, it chose me to be its father . . . I should have never forgiven myself if I had repelled its advances."

Rose was probably as fastidious as her father; nevertheless, her compassion was such that of deliberate choice she determined to devote the rest of her life to giving help to destitute sufferers from cancer. Today, such people would presumably be taken care of in a free city hospital, and even then a few patients were received without charge at the Memorial Hospital. To equip herself for her work she went there as an unpaid assistant to the nurses, for she had no idea as how best to bandage suppurating sores on the faces and bodies of these sufferers. Also, she had to inure herself to the faint but nauseous smell that such sores give off. It was a heroic decision, and she stuck to it until she herself died.

A worker at one of the so-called charities told her that she was distressing herself needlessly and that it would be difficult to find a case of genuine destitution. Another told her that two dollars a year was considered quite enough for a family on relief, adding: "Well, in New York we average a bit more than that." Rose knew that destitute sufferers from cancer were allowed to rot in any damp basement or hole they could find. If nobody else would look after these unfortunates, she would—and her treatment of them would be so tender that the poor would praise it highly.

Eventually, she took an apartment on 1 Scammel Street, a few small dark dirty rooms in which every window was broken. Yet it was the discomfort and inconvenience of the place that decided Rose; its one advantage was that the rent was negligible and that the room she occupied had a little window high up through which a salt breeze blew from the harbor; when the moon shone through, the scene was almost magical. And when she woke in the morning the grimy bedroom was radiant with the sun. With joyous heart she set about scrubbing the floors until she made the place presentable.

At first she was terrified by the kind of people she saw on the streets; their faces seemed so cruel and selfish. But soon her fear disappeared; these people were no different from others, except that they were poor and wretched. She told herself: "Well, my dear, you have set out to love everybody and to make everyone love each other. Of course, you can do very little, and you are as stupid as you can be. But the moment we set ourselves free from selfishness and sloth, everybody is refreshed. It works wonders—just as though God had brushed you aside and said, 'I am here.' "

Rose noticed, too, that these people lived as much as possible in the open air, and learned the reason: their rooms were too close, too full of the odors of human flesh and sweat. They even slept outside in the summer—on the fire escapes. Moreover, every little girl seemed to be carrying a baby as a doll, and if her mother did not have one, she borrowed a baby from another woman. Yet whenever a hurdy-gurdy started to play, these same little girls would at once deposit the babies somewhere and begin to dance. As for continuous noise—the elevated railway, horse-drawn trucks, the scream of a parrot or the wail of a cat—these people apparently enjoyed the uproar in which they lived, the only lull coming between midnight and four in the morning. There was not much else for them to enjoy except the beer; Rose decided at once that it was "bad" beer—the slum saloons sold only that which was cheap. Though she had an understandable prejudice against alcohol in any form, even against beer, she later found that the pain of cancer sufferers could be relieved by ale.

As she now had a small apartment, she took into it an old

woman, who, after six months at Memorial Hospital, had been dismissed as inoperable; the centre of her face was almost eaten away. Yet she was most anxious to help Rose in little ways, and in the evening she was most entertaining with her Irish tales. When Rose came down with pneumonia, it was this old woman who hurried out for a nurse, and who, after being told what to do by this nurse and a doctor, took charge of the situation. One of Rose's former friends who came to see her wondered how, with her refinement and appreciation of beauty, she could look at that face without shuddering. The answer returned was: "Perhaps it's because I love her. Sometimes I wonder whether I'm worthy of her love."

Rose knew when she went to Scammel Street that the building was soon to be pulled down by the city authorities. But she found another house nearby at 668 Water Street, a place that seemed palatial after the apartment, though it, too, was in the slums. There several kind-hearted young women came to help her and, though most of them left, finding the life too hard and disgusting, one of them was her right hand for the rest of her life and continued the work after Rose's death. This was Alice Huber—who was to become Sister Rose. She was the daughter of a Kentucky doctor and was a painter with a good position in an art school. Everything about the house on Water Street filled her with loathing and writing years later about her first day there she said that the memory of the frightful sore she dressed then still made her feel sick. But she disregarded her revulsion, believing that God wanted her to help the handsome red-headed woman of forty who was toiling so cheerfully for the cancerous poor.

By now, Mrs. Lathrop was beginning to attract some attention, so that by means of donations from friends she was able on May 1, 1899, to buy a house for $9,500 on 426 Cherry Street, which she named St. Rose's Free Home. St. Rose of Lima had been chosen, rather whimsically, as Rose Hawthorne's patron, while she was still a child, by the beautiful transcendentalist Elizabeth Hoar. Rose herself became attached to the name and the person, even naming the branch of Dominican Sisters she founded the Congregation of St. Rose of Lima.

That a more definite religious character was given to the undertaking was due to a chance call in February, 1899, by a young Dominican priest. He had gone to Water Street, as the move to Cherry Street had not yet been made, to thank the unknown ladies who, he had heard, had been helping a poor woman who belonged to the Dominican parish on Lexington Avenue. He could hardly believe that anybody could be living in such a hovel. But he was impressed by the piety of Mrs. Lathrop and Miss Huber and when his attention was caught by a statuette of St. Rose of Lima, he asked: "Why don't you become Dominican tertiaries like her?"

When they became Dominican tertiaries, Rose and Alice adopted a linen dress, with a cap resembling that of the New York Sisters of Charity. When they presented themselves to Archbishop Corrigan in this attire, he was distinctly annoyed, and refused them permission to wear what he saw was a semi-religious dress. Only upon a second appeal did the Servants of Relief, as they had begun to call themselves, obtain the archbishop's consent.

Rose Hawthorne Lathrop had taken the name of Alphonsa, allowing Alice Huber to become Sister Rose, on September 14, 1899. Although they were not permitted to wear the Dominican habit, they tried to live a more religious life, saying the Little Office of Our Lady in English and devoting regular periods to meditation and prayer. But they had to go to the parish church for Mass, and it was not until Christmas Day that Mass was said for the first time in the little chapel of St. Rose's Free Home. They were getting closer to constituting themselves a community. After they had been tertiaries for a year Archbishop Corrigan allowed them to wear the white wool of St. Dominic.

Then an opportunity occurred, quite unexpectedly, for them to buy a much larger house north of White Plains in Westchester County. It had once been a summer hotel named Tecumseh, but had passed into the possession of a group of French Dominicans. They were now about to give it up. The price asked—$28,000 for a house of sixty rooms and nine acres of land—was ridiculously low, but seemed staggering to the tertiaries from Cherry Street. However, as the priests asked only $1,000 as down payment, Sister Alphonsa, in spite of Sister Rose's fears that they would never be able to meet the heavy carrying charges, felt that this was much too good a chance to neglect.

The arrangement was that Mother Alphonsa would move some of her patients there, as well as the novices they were now receiving. Though superior general of the little community, she would act as novice mistress—a dual activity no longer permitted. Though the structure at Hawthorne, as the village is now called, was of wood, and being long-stretched out (which made it look like a ship stranded on the top of a hill), was hard to heat, this new home would seem a paradise after Cherry Street. That place was not given up, as it was needed for the cancerous poor of the city, who remained there in charge of Sister Rose until they could be sent to Hawthorne.

In the rules as approved by the archbishop three are of special interest. One was that the Servants of Relief were never to wear rubber gloves while dressing cancer sores. Another was that the knife was never to be used, for only inoperable cases were accepted. The third and most important of the three was that only completely destitute patients were eligible for admission. Mother Alphonsa well realized that if even a few paying patients were received there would be a temptation to admit others, and the result would be that eventually the destitute would be crowded out. From time to time an attempt was made to get around this regulation by giving a handsome donation to Rosary Hill (the new name of the home), as that, technically, would not be paying hospital charges, but Mother Alphonsa was adamant against such a subterfuge. In any case, this was not a hospital but a home; it contained no "patients," only guests. A fourth rule might also be noted: there was to be no age limit, so that even children were sometimes admitted. And there was no discrimination on account of religion or color. Mother Alphonsa never even refused anything to a tramp who asked for help, sometimes having eight or nine derelicts for dinner and giving them shelter over night. She often vowed to throw the next tramp out, but she never had the heart to do so.

The two homes—in New York City and at Hawthorne—were supported entirely by charitable donations, plus the fruit and vegetables and eggs from the chickens produced at Rosary Hill. What the expenses were for September, 1901, we know from the accounts kept: at Hawthorne they amounted to $226.17 and at Cherry Street to $83.17. Naturally, the expenses shot up when the furnaces were lighted. At the start the "guests" were few. Today the numbers are large, especially as the original homes—which soon became crowded—have been replaced by more substantial buildings, that on Cherry Street by a commodious brick building on the lower part of the East Drive. In each place, though death strikes frequently, those received usually live a considerably longer time than do cancer patients in a hospital, and anybody admitted is free to remain for the rest of his life.

The crown of the work was the building of two larger homes. That in New York was the result of an offer in 1911 of $25,000 from a priest there, on condition that Mother Alphonsa would equal it. This she managed to do by appealing to other potential benefactors. And using the same methods she contrived by 1926 to collect $150,000, which Cardinal

Hayes agreed was enough for her to start building the new Rosary Hill Home, which then cost $317,000.

Mother Alphonsa did not live to see its completion, for on July 9, 1926, she died in her sleep. Sister Rose had seen her only the previous day, and she had seemed very well then. And shortly before this she had been visited by her brother Julian Hawthorne, then hale and hearty and looking rather like the son of their father's old friend of the same name, Oliver Wendell Holmes. Mother Alphonsa herself was seventy-seven. Despite her lack of success in the earlier years of her life, in her last ones she attained a far greater success —her work for destitute sufferers from cancer.

XX: Miriam Teresa Demjanovich

(1901–1927)

Miriam Teresa Demjanovich is, probably, the least famous of those in this book, yet she may become one of the most famous if she is canonized. One reason for introducing her is that, though a member of a group founded only for active work, she proved herself a mystic. One might suppose that she was completely out of place there, and, indeed, only went to these Sisters because the purely contemplative Carmelites had refused her because of her health. Yet, though some members of her community think she should have joined a contemplative order, it may well be that her special vocation was to infuse a contemplative spirit among nuns absorbed by activity. Yet a second reason is the fact that she died technically a member of one of the Eastern Churches that are in communion with Rome. This has great significance in our day, when the Holy See is making special efforts to foster those rites.

Over seventy years ago there came to this country from Bardejov in the Carpathians a young man named Alexander Demjanovich and his bride Johanna Szuchy. Alexander was a highly skilled maker of custom-built shoes, and in this trade he worked for a while in New York City, before moving to Bayonne, New Jersey. There were a number of their fellow countrymen there, whereas the Demjanoviches had felt somewhat lost in New York. Moreover, in Bayonne there was a Catholic Church of an Eastern rite, with whose liturgy and customs they were more familiar than with the Latin Mass.

At Bayonne they settled in what is called the Constable Hook district. That part of the city contained a number of oil refineries and paint factories, which during the day emitted unpleasant odors; rents were low there as a result. But in such a location few customers could be found for custom-built shoes, so before long Demjanovich opened a small shop in one of the front rooms of his house and stocked it with ready-made shoes, as these could be more easily disposed of. Of an easy-going disposition, he too frequently gave credit to customers from whom he should have demanded cash. The result was that he found that he had $600 in bad debts, and therefore turned to another trade—that of a cooper of oil barrels. As he was so skilled in fitting the barrel staves that not a drop of oil escaped, he never lacked employment, at wages that were good for those days—about twenty dollars a week. It was in this work that he was engaged for the next sixteen years.

Teresa, the youngest of the Demjanovich children—there were two other daughters and two sons—was born in Bayonne on March 26, 1901. She was baptized five days later, and was confirmed immediately afterwards by the priest who had administered baptism.

At this time the Demjanoviches were attending the local church of an Eastern rite, whose priest, of course, was married. Teresa's first childhood friend was the priest's daughter. But her brother Charles, so close to her in age that he was often taken to be her twin, was more of a companion. With him, when they had grown old enough, Teresa would play baseball in a vacant lot—probably not very well because of her poor eyesight, but at least enthusiastically. They used to tip-toe out of the house very early in the morning, when the air was free of the obnoxious odors that came later in the day.

Teresa was prepared for her first Communion by her father, though a lay teacher and sometimes the priest also gave instruction. In fact, after she began attendance at the public school, this teacher would gather all the children for a daily "Sunday School." The fasts in the Eastern Catholic

Church are many and severe, and holy days of obligation frequent. These, like Sundays, first of all had a purely religious significance. But after the religious duties had been carried out, there would be a pleasant social gathering in the Demjanovich house, in the afternoon, attended by relatives and friends.

Their own church had no parochial school, and those of the Latin rite were too crowded to admit outsiders. As a result, all the Demjanovich children went to public schools. Teresa's piety was kindled by what she first learned when she was in the Eastern-rite parish. It would have continued to develop there had not her family moved from the Constable Hook district into a better section of Bayonne. Then, with the exception of the father, they found it more convenient to assist at Mass at the nearer Roman-rite church.

This now brought her, for the first time in her life, into contact with Sisters, for there were no nuns who observed the Rule of St. Basil in Bayonne. The idea of entering a convent seems to have occurred to her when she went on to St. Elizabeth's College at Morristown after she had graduated at the local public high school.

Just how she was able to pay her college fees does not appear. The move into a better house indicates that the family fortunes had improved, but this was mainly due to the fact that her eldest brother and sister were working and now able to contribute to the family needs. One sister held a good position as secretary to the assistant superintendent of schools; the other went into training as a hospital nurse.

In due time Teresa obtained her degree at St. Elizabeth's. Her teachers recall that she was not scintillatingly brilliant, but was, rather, a student who conscientiously prepared herself for all her classes. At college, and even during her high-school days, she wrote a certain amount of verse, which was technically competent and very sincere. Teresa had no illusions as to its merit, and was devoid of literary ambitions.

She was happy enough during her four years at college, but acquired only a few close friends. This does not mean that she was unpopular, but merely that some of her fellow students set her down as a bit "odd," chiefly because her outlook came so strongly from her upbringing among Eastern-rite Catholics. Moreover, she was not good at games. Nor was she pretty. Her appearance was not improved by the thick-lensed glasses she had to wear. Her clothes were inexpensive and often made by herself. Perhaps everything can be summed up by saying that the young are inclined to be conventional, and Teresa did not conform to the accepted pattern. Her seriousness and conscientiousness were fully appreciated only by those who came to know her well. But she did have a sense of humor, and some of the light verse she contributed to the college annual, the *Elizabethan,* was rightly admired.

Teresa and one other girl were graduated *summa cum laude*. This is all the more creditable because, having gone to St. Elizabeth's with only two years of high-school Latin, she had to take a "make up" course privately from one of the Sisters.

Upon her return to Bayonne, Teresa accepted a teaching position at St. Aloysius's Academy, conducted by the New Jersey Sisters of Charity. Her subjects were English and Latin and drawing, but she was a poor disciplinarian, being too soft-hearted to exercise sufficient firmness and therefore found teaching highly distasteful.

Teresa was thinking and praying a good deal about her vocation, and intended to join a contemplative order. Therefore, accompanied by her brother Charles, who recently had been ordained a priest, she applied for admission to the Carmelites in the Bronx. Their superior did not give an outright refusal, but as she noticed that Teresa's eyes were so weak as to flicker, she suggested that she return in two years. Teresa knew there was no hope of any improvement, and she had to take the suggestion as a final refusal. Moreover, as her father's health had begun to fail, she felt she could not leave him just then. The care of the household accordingly fell on her shoulders. Not until his death a couple of years later was she free to follow her vocation.

Teresa's decision to enter at St. Elizabeth's was made suddenly, while she was on a visit to see some of her friends among the Sisters. She was somewhat reluctant to join a community whose main work was teaching, though they also conducted hospitals. However, she could be practically certain that she would be assigned to the college department, and she fancied that more mature students would be easier to handle than the mischievous imps of St. Aloysius.

Yet Teresa knew something about the history of the Sisters of Charity. They were at first only a band of strong country girls gathered to help St. Vincent de Paul's Ladies of Charity —a group not expected to perform rough and heavy tasks. For a long time they did not have a habit, or take religious names, but simply wore the kind of clothes to which peasant girls were accustomed. This was a kind of uniform, but was not intended to be a religious dress. Up to that time all nuns were strictly cloistered, but Monsieur Vincent made it clear to his daughters that "their convent is the sick room, their chapel the parish church, their cloister the streets of the city." When they were provided with a rule, they were to take vows only for one year; they had to be renewed annually, if they wished to remain. They were to consider themselves called to the active life, and, though it goes without saying that that life derives its merit from prayer, contemplation as such is not stressed, though visionaries have now and then appeared among them, such as St. Catherine Labouré. Nevertheless, the distinctive vocation of the Sister of Charity is performing corporal works of mercy.

The spiritual director of both the novices and the professed Sisters at St. Elizabeth's was a Benedictine from St. Mary's Abbey, Newark. This Fr. Benedict Bradley gave weekly conferences and spiritual direction to the community. He was so struck with Teresa's exalted spirituality that he asked her, even though she was only a novice, to write the conferences which he read to the Sisters as though he had composed them in full, though he did no more than throw in a few impromptu "asides" as he went along. Nobody except the superior was informed that Teresa was the real author; and nobody so much as suspected it, even if a few discerning souls, reading over the mimeographed conference, would sometimes say, "Now *that* does not sound very like Father Benedict!" The secret was safely kept, even from the novice mistress, until Teresa's death, when Fr. Bradley put a notice on the bulletin board at the chapel door. These conferences were published in 1948 under the title *Greater Perfection.*

The central theme of these conferences was that the Sister of Charity should aim at a higher spirituality; in short, at a "greater perfection." Never was it suggested that active work should be renounced in favor of contemplation. All that Teresa was trying to say was that one should not be too much engrossed, like Martha, in bustling occupations, especially not when Christ arrived as a guest. Teresa's novice mistress naturally discouraged those under her charge from reading too many mystical works. These were excellent for those called to the contemplative life, but not for those, like the Sisters of Charity who were in the active life. She did not, of course, actually prohibit the reading of St. Teresa of Avila or St. John of the Cross, but she was uneasy about novices like Miriam Teresa (who had tacked on the Miriam to her baptismal name) who seemed to be becoming too engrossed in such methods of prayer. Teresa's superior did not see any real clash in her way of acting; otherwise, she would have replaced Fr. Bradley with a spiritual director of a different type. It was with her full knowledge and consent that Teresa wrote, in a little room opposite her office, her series of conferences.

Teresa was more mature, even in years, when she entered

than were most of the other novices; when she was still a child she obtained a great insight into spiritual things, and this insight increased during her college years and after. Finally, under the careful direction of Fr. Bradley, a man quick to perceive her potentialities, she developed still further. He did not attempt to press her into a cast-iron mould, but left her to follow the promptings of the Holy Spirit, with only a minimum of direction from himself.

A year before Teresa's death there were indications that her health had begun to fail, and this to a great extent was due to the strain she was under. There were at least two spells of sickness, neither very serious in itself, but disturbing in view of her condition of general debility. The novice mistress allowed her to go to bed for a few days in the infirmary, but found it hard to believe that any of her novices could have much wrong with them. At last what was called a quinsy sore throat, nothing worse than the inflammation of the tonsils, necessitated a minor operation, and for this Miriam Teresa was taken to the Sisters' hospital at Paterson, New Jersey. On the last day of 1926 she returned to St. Elizabeth's, but was so weak that she had to hold on to the wall as she dragged herself upstairs. Completely exhausted, she again had to go into the infirmary, and even the superior, when she visited her there, told the novice, with a touch of unusual asperity, "Pull yourself together." Talking about this to Fr. Bradley, Miriam Teresa could but comment, "Father, for a long time there has been nothing to pull."

The spiritual director passed this on to Miriam Teresa's priest brother, and he sent word to their sister, Anne, who was now a nurse. When Anne arrived she insisted on taking her back in a taxi to the hospital. There her chart read: "Physical and nervous exhaustion, with myocarditis and acute appendicitis." Even so it was not decided until March 26 that an appendectomy would be necessary.

But Miriam Teresa knew that she was dying, though the

doctors were still talking about building her up for the operation. Fr. Demjanovich now asked the Superior at St. Elizabeth's if Teresa might be allowed to take her vows at once. Permission was given, and Fr. Benedict received her vows in May. It was just after this that the too long deferred operation occurred. Immediately afterwards there was a turn for the worse; for peritonitis struck and on May 8, 1927, Miriam Teresa died.

Even before Miriam Teresa's body was taken out of the hospital at Paterson the first of what seemed to be miracles wrought through her intercession occurred, and there was another at her funeral. Still more extraordinary happenings took place later, though as to whether any of them was a miracle in the sense defined by the Holy See must be left to the decision of the Congregation of Rites.

XXI: Alfred E. Smith

(1873–1943)

Catholic Irish politicians have often been supposed, even with proof to the contrary, to be all notoriously corrupt. That this is true in some cases is not to be denied, though the great majority of venal politicians America has known have not belonged to any one race or faith. It should be quite unnecessary to begin by saying that Alfred E. Smith was as unlike the standard caricature of a politician as it is possible to be.

But he was a Tammany man, and Tammany Hall had often been considered a synonym for the worst kind of corrupt city politics. A word should be said about this. In the first place it should be remembered that Tammany Hall, or "St. Tammany" as it was once derisively called, was an organization that antedated the American Revolution. At first it operated in federal or state matters, only later gaining control of New York City. Its worst phase was under "Boss" Tweed, who, incidentally, was not an Irishman.

After the downfall of Tweed in 1871, Tammany experienced a series of purges, increasingly thorough-going, under a succession of Irish bosses. The greatest force in this reforming process was Alfred E. Smith, who began as a district leader in New York City before rising to higher office. Though he remained a sachem, he was never the head of Tammany, that position being obtained in 1924 by Judge Olvany who, with Smith's co-operation, purged Tammany still further.

Alfred E. Smith was born in the Fourth Ward in the Lower East Side of New York on December 30, 1873, of humble parentage. The family neighbors were predominantly Irish, though with many Italians and Jews among them, and a smattering of Germans, Slavs and Greeks. The control of the district was in the hands of Tammany, and after a somewhat sketchy education—he said of himself that he was a graduate of the Fulton Fish Market—Smith, as was almost inevitable of a young man of his type, entered politics in a small way. Yet, from the outset, the rise of what Hapgood and Moskowitz call this "fun-loving, warm-hearted lover of his fellow human beings" was assured.

Though politics came, even in his early youth, to absorb nearly all of Smith's free time, he was still able to indulge his liking for amateur theatricals in the dramatic society connected with his parish church, St. James's. This interest never left him; even when he was Governor of New York State he was a member of the famous cast which included Judge Nolan and Mayor Walker in a production of *The Shaughraun*. As he wrote in his autobiography: "I was interested in amateur theatricals before I was old enough to play before a grown-up audience . . . The garret of the Smith house was often turned into a miniature theatre. With the boys of the neighborhood for a cast and my sister and her girl friends to act the feminine parts, many a reproduction of current drama and many a home-made play were enacted there." He sometimes took the leading role; sometimes that of the villain, as in *The Shaughraun*. This was staged for two evenings in a theatre on the Bowery, and again, when the parish of St. James was in need of funds, in the basement of the church.

This sort of thing was undoubtedly of great aid in Smith's career as a public speaker, and though he never was what can be called an orator, he made himself a speaker of remarkable force and forthrightness. Whenever possible, each speech dealt with a single topic, so that his audience would not be confused by having to take in a number of points; everything was compact and neat. He never seemed to need more than a few notes jotted down on an old envelope; for his well-stored, orderly mind these sufficed. Though not a great general reader, he read such works as he felt he ought to know. Most of his time had to be given to a careful study of the complicated reports that came to him, and he was to show himself a great master of detail.

Busy though he was in the days when he had a city district to look after, he found time to court a dark-haired, rather reserved girl named Catherine Dunn, whose home was in the Bronx. He used to visit her on 170th Street, riding a bicycle from downtown, but wearing a derby hat, a cut-away coat, striped trousers, four-in-hand tie and the kind of a collar known as a "stand-up." By that time he was earning good wages and so was able to present himself to Miss Dunn in what seemed a fashionable appearance. They were married on May 6, 1900. He took her to live in a house on Oliver Street, and their first son was born on January 26, 1901, and their eldest daughter, Emily, now Mrs. John A. Warner, eleven months later. These were followed by three other children. The marriage proved eminently happy.

In politics young Al Smith was definitely a product of the "machine," and there has probably never been a man his equal in the handling of the immigrant population, which reached its peak at the turn of the century. At the same time it must be said that he was from the outset an exponent of soundly progressive political thought, and he showed himself expert, especially as his position and experience enabled him to put his ideas into effect, in bringing about practical improvements. Hapgood and Moskowitz, commenting on the singular concreteness of his mind, write: "Never was a brain more specific. He does not start from an interest in general principles and proceed to an interest in detail. He starts with the problem in front of him, and the mastery of that concrete problem is what leads him to his general principles." In short, Smith was not a political theorist, but, in the best sense, a practical politician.

Smith's Catholicism was not only regular and exact but unobtrusive. The late Senator Wagner, in the chapter he contributed to *The Road to Damascus,* edited by Fr. John A. O'Brien, named Smith as the man who influenced him most in the direction of the Church. Smith never thrust his own religious convictions down Wagner's throat, but it was as natural for him to talk about God's will as it was to discuss a state budget or a program for the development of public power. The two men roomed together when they were first in Albany. They arrived there together very late at night and had to be up again three hours later, but Wagner, who got under the covers at once, saw Smith, rosary in hand, kneeling by his bed to say his night prayers.

He was elected assemblyman for the first time in 1903, when he was thirty, and was selected to run only after others had refused to do so. He was himself to attribute his success "to just being around"; but, while that no doubt helped a great deal, he was already known to be a man of ability and character, and this counted for more.

At Albany he soon made his mark in the Assembly, all the more so because he had the courage to emerge (though tactfully and quietly) out of the "machine." While always thoroughly loyal to the Democratic Party, he was cast in no rigid mold, as most politicians are, but thought carefully and clearly for himself. Moreover, while most politicians cultivate geniality—too often a *fausse bonhomie*—this engaging young man made people feel that his kind interest in them was genuine. He was therefore trusted as well as liked—not only by Democrats but by such staunch Republicans as Elihu Root and James W. Wadsworth.

It was the custom to reward New York Democratic assemblymen who had given faithful service to the party. Smith was not, like so many assemblymen, a lawyer with a private practice, so he had only his assemblyman's salary of $1,500 upon which to support his wife and children. As even in those days this was not nearly enough, Boss Murphy put Smith up to run against the Republican who held the office of sheriff. As the sheriff received fees which amounted to more than $50,000 a year, this office was a great plum. When the Citizens' Union, an independent reform association, declared for him, his election was assured. Not only was Smith now put on "easy street" at last, his way was prepared to still higher office. In the 1917 election he might have become Mayor of New York had not Boss Murphy wished to placate Hearst, by backing his protégé, Hylan. Instead, Smith obtained a position on the Port Authority, and the efficient work he did there led him to the governorship of the Empire state.

Smith proved himself to be a governor of a new sort. His was a sound business administration, but one in which efficiency showed that it had a heart. Smith consistently battled for the underdog, and he was completely free of any favoritism towards his co-religionists. His cabinet (the first ever to sit in the state) contained only one Catholic; his fellow members were thirteen Protestants and one Jew. Yet he was only carrying out Catholic principles in naming the most capable and honest men he could find, or, for that matter, principles which anyone in power ought to put into practice. This might have been remembered during his presidential campaign of 1928, but was not.

Because he had made a great name for himself as governor, he was put forward for the Democratic nomination for president in 1924. He failed to obtain this, being beaten not so much by McAdoo (who also failed to get the nomination) as by the Ku Klux Klan, so that after an inordinately long convention John W. Davis, an able lawyer and a highly respected man, was chosen but did not prove a strong candidate. It was at this convention that "East Side, West Side" became Smith's campaign song. It was due only to the fact that the band could not think of any New York State song that it played this in compliment to the man whose name had just been put forward.

Perhaps it was just as well that Smith was not nominated that year; no Democrat and certainly no Catholic would have had the slightest chance. By the time of the next convention the Klan was somewhat discredited, but, though it was not able to prevent Smith's nomination, it was strong enough to throw considerable weight against his election. There is no need to attribute solely to his Catholicism the defeat of Governor Smith when he ran for the presidency. Ex-President Hoover argues in his *Memoirs* that had the Democratic candidate been a Protestant he would have been even more decisively beaten. And D. W. Brogan has remarked: "There is no evidence that this mixture of religious zeal [among anti-Catholic bigots], hallucinations, ecclesiastical competition and, in some, a taste for sanctified pornography made any great difference. Only a miracle could have defeated any Republican candidate in that year and Mr. Hoover, as the leading businessman in politics, was a very strong candidate in the last years of the uncontested rule of the business community."

Though he obtained a greater number of popular votes than any defeated candidate had ever received up to that time, the number of his electoral votes was only 88 as against 444 for Hoover. The "Solid South" cracked—partly because Smith was a Catholic; partly because his name was identified with their picture of Tammany; partly because (while acknowledged to be a very able and honest man) he was thought to be a diamond very much in the rough; partly because of the whispering campaign against Mrs. Smith that was absolutely disgraceful; and partly because of Smith's courageous stand against prohibition. But while all these factors operated, nothing was so detrimental to Smith as that he was opposed by Hoover, the man who, it was believed, would lead the country to a prosperity still greater than that of the Coolidge boom.

About prohibition, which Hoover had called "an experiment noble in intention" (which amounted to an admission that it had failed, and the admission was confirmed by the Wickersham Report), Smith, disregarding the Democratic platform, spoke out so plainly as to pave the way for repeal. For this some prohibitionists took their revenge by circulating reports, in which there was not a word of truth, that Smith had several times been seen drunk—the only charge against him which he took the trouble to refute in his autobiography.

Governor Smith, in an open letter to the editor published in the *Atlantic Monthly* for May, 1927, answered the question raised by the well-known lawyer Charles C. Marshall in the preceding issue as to whether there was any conflict between the governor's loyalty to the Catholic Church and his loyalty to the United States. Smith of course asserted, as would any American Catholic, that such a conflict is unthinkable. "The essence of my faith," he wrote, "is built upon the Commandments of God. The law of the land is built upon the Commandments of God." He went on to say: "You as a lawyer will probably agree that the office of Chief Justice of the United States is second not even to that of the President in its influence on the national development and policy. That court by its interpretation of the Federal Constitution is a check not only upon the President himself but upon Congress as well. During one-fourth of its history it has been presided over by two Catholics, Roger Brooke Taney and Edward Douglass White. No one has suggested that the official conduct of either of these men was affected by any unwarranted religious influence or that religion played with them any other part than it should play in the life of every God-fearing man."

The Democratic candidate for the presidency in 1928 displayed little if any bitterness about the outcome of the election, but he believed that in 1932 he should have been given another chance, for in that year almost any Democrat (even perhaps a Catholic) could have beaten a Hoover who was now called responsible for the depression. But in 1932 the Democratic Convention was frightened of the idea of putting forward a Catholic a second time. Instead, Franklin D. Roosevelt was nominated and elected.

Smith had not made any active candidacy for the nomination, but had merely let it be known that he was "available." Not until the New Deal was advocated did he announce that he was "going to take a walk." As he put it at the Jefferson Day dinner, this was, in his opinion, "no time for demagogues." Whether Smith was right or wrong in his opinion of the brilliant and aristocratic Roosevelt, a great many other people shared his views, and looked askance at the political policies of the New Deal.

After his failure to be nominated, Al Smith, at the invitation of his campaign manager John J. Rascob, became president of the corporation that erected the Empire State Building, at a salary of $50,000 a year. The lad who had started as a summoner of truck drivers on the lower East Side had come a long way. He had made a great reputation for himself in politics, and this was not diminished by what happened in 1928, for his sterling character was universally recognized. It was also recognized that he had given New York State a first-rate business administration; therefore, it was inevitable that his business talents should be utilized in a new field.

Smith took little part in politics after this, but devoted himself actively to the management of the Empire State Building. His nature was too ebullient, his character too magnanimous, for him to be unduly downcast because the greatest ambition of his life had failed. His popularity was undiminished; he remained the same charming, humorous and affable man that he had always been. Nor did he yield to the temptation to which a smaller man might have succumbed of allowing his success in business to make him arrogant; instead, he was as modest and as likeable as ever, plain Al Smith.

Sorrows came to him, of course, during his last years, as they come to all men. On May 4, 1943, his beloved Katie died, and after that his own health began to fail. Yet his high spirits remained; we hear of his singing old songs and even dancing a jig at his eldest daughter's birthday party on July 25, at Southampton, Long Island, the summer home of the Warners. However, the next morning he would not eat any breakfast and confessed that he was not feeling at all well. All the same he went back to his desk and tried to keep on with his work. Emily Warner had driven him back to New York, but a few days later he had to go to the hospital. There his bearing was as matter-of-fact as ever.

That very night he took a turn for the worse and the priest was summoned. Smith asked: "Am I dying, Father?" to which the priest could only say: "Yes." The calm reply was: "Then start the act of contrition." He was given the last sacraments, after which he sank into unconsciousness, and on the morning of Friday, October 4, 1943, died. His was a death completely in keeping with his life: simple, devoted and unspectacular. He had accomplished so much that there is no need to grieve that he did not have the chance to use whatever greater talents he possessed. As it is, his probity and patriotism will always be an inspiration to Americans of every creed.

Bibliographical Notes

I: St. Isaac Jogues

By far the most complete and satisfactory life of Jogues is Francis Talbot, S.J., *Saint among Savages* (New York, 1935); it may be regarded as definitive. *The Jesuit Relations* should also be consulted. But as the 73 volumes as edited by R. G. Thwaites are likely to be inaccessible to most readers, the one-volume condensation under the same title made by Edna Kenton (New York, 1925; revised, 1954) will probably serve well enough. F. X. Charlevoix, S.J., *Histoire de la Nouvelle France* (Eng. trans. by J. G. Shea as *History of New France,* 6 vols., New York, 1866) is perhaps best for the general background. Thomas Campbell, S.J., *Pioneer Priests of North America,* 2 vols. (New York, 1910, 1913) and John J. Wynne, S.J., *The Jesuit Martyrs of North America* (New York, 1925) should also be consulted. A pioneer and classic study is Francis Parkman *The Jesuits in North America* (Boston, 1868). Though the author's Puritan prejudices now and then peep out, they do not unduly protrude themselves.

II: Père Marquette

Père Marquette by Agnes Repplier (New York, 1929), is probably the best biography so far. The most scholarly study is *The Jolliet-Marquette Expedition* by Francis Borgia Steck, O.F.M. (Glendale, Calif., 1928), though its findings have not received general acceptance. Most of the other biographies may be safely disregarded, though mention might be made of *Father Marquette* by Samuel Hedges (New York, 1903). The bibliographical note about *The Jesuit Relations* for Chapter I also applies here.

III: Kateri Tekakwitha

The basic material for the life of Kateri Tekakwitha is contained in the *Positio of the Historical Section of the Sacred Congregation of Rites on the Introduction of the Cause for Beatification and Canonization and on the Virtues of the Servant of God Katherine Tekakwitha, the Lily of the Mohawks,* ed. by Robert E. Holland, S.J. (New York, 1940). This contains Père Pierre Cholonec's "The Life of Katherine Tegakoiita, First Iroquois Virgin" (pp. 239-335) and Père Claude Chauchetière's "The Life of Katherine Tekakwitha, Now Known as the Holy Savage" (pp. 111-211). Subsequent writers have made shrewd observations or given a fuller ethnic background but all have found the *Positio* indispensable. By far the best of the recent Lives are those by Marie Cecilia Buehrle, *Kateri of the Mohawks* (Milwaukee, 1954), Edward Lecompte, S.J., *The Glory of the Mohawks* (Milwaukee, 1944), and Daniel Sargent, *Catherine Tekakwitha* (New York, 1936).

IV: Junípero Serra

The basic life of Serra was that written by his friend Francisco Palóu. This was translated by C. Scott Williams and published at Pasadena, Calif., in 1913. A more accurate translation was published in 1955 by Maynard J. Geiger, O.F.M. Fr. Geiger also has in preparation a translation of Serra's letters and a definitive life. Other amply documented lives are Charles J. G. Maximim Piette's *L'Evocation de Junipero Serra* and *Le Secret de Junipero Serra,* each in two volumes (Washington, 1946, 1948). "Popular" lives have been written by Abigail H. Finch (1904), Agnes Repplier (1933), Theodore Maynard (1954) and Omer Englebert (1956). The best books on the California missions are those by Fr. Zephyrim Englehardt (4 vols., San Francisco, 1908-15), though those by George Wharton James (1915) and John A. Berger (1941) have merits. Herbert E. Bolton has translated and edited several of the diaries of Serra's contemporaries in California and also Palóu's *Historical Memoirs of New California.*

V: John Carroll

Volume I of John Gilmary Shea, *History of the Catholic Church in the United States* (4 vols., New York, 1886-92), is really a life of John Carroll. This, however, was largely superseded by Peter Guilday, *Life and Times of John Carroll* (New York, 1922), just as Monsignor Guilday has been corrected on several points by the more recent biography by Annabelle M. Melville. To these might be added Ellen Hart Smith, *Charles Carroll of Carrollton* (Cambridge, Mass., 1942), and Thomas F. Meehan's *Catholic Builders of the Nation,* Vol. I (New York, 1923).

VI: Pierre Toussaint

The earliest biography of Toussaint is that by Helen Farnham Lee (Boston, 1854), whose name does not appear on the title page and who draws largely upon the notes left by Mrs. Philip J. Schuyler, who had it in mind to write a book herself but who died fifteen months before Toussaint. As both ladies knew him well, a warm intimacy is shown that others naturally could not achieve. The most complete and up-to-date life is by Arthur and Elizabeth Sheehan, *Pierre Toussaint* (New York, 1955). Henry Binsse, "Pierre Toussaint, a Catholic Uncle Tom," *Historical Records and Studies,* Vol. XII (June, 1918), and Leo Ryan, "Pierre Toussaint, God's Image Carved in Ebony," *Historical Records and Studies,* Vol. XXV, are of secondary importance.

VII: Benedict Joseph Flaget

The following works on the expansion of the Church along the frontier are of significant help:

Baunard, Abbé, *The Life of Mother Duchesne* (Roehampton, England, 1879).

Erskine, Marjory, *Mother Philippine Duchesne* (New York, 1926).

Fox, Sister Columba, *The Life of the Right Reverend John Baptist David* (New York, 1925).

Keppel, Leopoldina Olivia, *Blessed Philippine Duchesne* (London and New York, 1940).

McAvoy, Thomas T., C.S.C., *The Catholic Church in Indiana* (New York, 1940).

Maes, Camillus P., *The Life of the Reverend Charles Nerinckx* (Cincinnati, 1880).

Mattingly, Sister M. Ramona, *The Catholic Church on the Kentucky Frontier* (Washington, D. C., 1937).

Maynard, Theodore, *The Reed and the Rock: Portrait of Simon Bruté* (New York, 1943).

O'Daniel, Victor F., O.P., *The Right Reverend Edward Dominic Fenwick* (Washington, D. C., 1920).

Schauinger, J. Herman, *Cathedrals in the Wilderness* (Milwaukee, 1952).

Spalding, Martin J., *Sketches of the Early Catholic Missions of Kentucky* (Louisville and Baltimore, 1844).

———, *Sketches of the Life, Times and Character of the Right Reverend Benedict Joseph Flaget* (Louisville, 1852).

Webb, Benjamin J., *The Centenary of Catholicity in Kentucky* (Louisville, 1884).

VIII: Mother Seton

By far the best biography is *Elizabeth Bayley Seton* by Annabelle M. Melville (New York, 1951). Prior to its appearance the best was that by Charles I. White, first published in Baltimore in 1853, but recently reissued in New York with some revisions. Hélène Bailly de Barberey is also very good. Her book, published in Paris in 1868, has been translated into English, with some new matter added, by Joseph B. Code and published in New York in 1927. My *Reed and the Rock* (New York, 1943) is primarily a portrait of Simon Bruté, but Mother Seton comes into it a good deal, and I was able to use some letters never published before, as photostats of these had just arrived from the Felicchi archives in Italy. *The Mountain* by Mary M. Meline and Edward F. X. Sweeny, Vol. I, contains some material about her. Finally, I should mention two privately printed collections of letters by Mother Seton and by Bishop Bruté made in 1884 and 1888. They were intended only for the use of the Sisters of Charity of Emmitsburg, but were opened to me for use in writing *The Reed and the Rock.*

IX: John England

The best biography is Peter Guilday, *The Life and Times of John England* (2 vols., New York, 1927). Another is J. L. O'Brien, *John England, Bishop of Charleston* (New York, 1934). The best edition of England's *Collected Works* is that edited by Archbishop Messmer (7 vols., Milwaukee, 1908). Also valuable are "The Life of Henry Conwell, Second Bishop of Philadelphia," by Martin I. J. Griffin and Lemuel B. Norton, *Records of the American Catholic Historical Society* (1917-18), and J. Herman Schauinger, *William Gaston, Carolinian* (Milwaukee, 1949).

X: Prince Gallitzin

The best written of the biographies is *The Life of Demetrius Augustine Gallitzin* by Sarah M. Brownson, daughter of Orestes Brownson. Peter Lemcke, *Life and Work of Prince Demetrius Augustine Gallitzin* (New York, 1940) is also well translated and has the advantage of having been produced by one immediately associated with Gallitzin. Daniel Sargent, *Mitri* (New York, 1945) draws upon some material not available to previous writers.

XI: John Hughes

The definitive life of Archbishop Hughes is still to be written; materials were gathered for one by Peter Guilday before his death, and are now the property of the Archdiocese of New York. Some information appears in early biographies by John G. Hazzard (New York, 1866) and by Monsignor Henry A. Brann, little more than a condensation of Hazzard; much about his student days is in Vol. I of *The Mountain,* by Mary M. Meline and Edward F. X. Sweeny. The only biography of Bishop Dubois, to whom Hughes became coadjutor, is Charles G. Herbermann, "The Rt. Rev. John Dubois, Third Bishop of New York," *Historical Records and Studies* (1900), pp. 278-385. Humphrey J. Desmond, *The Know Nothing Party* (Washington, 1919), and Ray Allen Billington, *The Protestant Crusade* (New York, 1938) are also valuable.

XII: Pierre De Smet

Bancroft, Hubert, *History of Oregon,* 2 vols. (San Francisco, 1886-88).

Chittenden, H. M., and A. T. Richardson, *Life, Letters and Travels of Father Pierre-Jean De Smet,* 4 vols. (New York, 1905).

De Smet, Pierre J., *Letters and Sketches, with a Narrative of a Year's Residence among the Indian Tribes of the Rocky Mountains* (Philadelphia, 1843).

———, *Oregon Missions and Travels in the Rocky Mountains in 1845-1846* (New York, 1847).

———, *Western Missions and Missionaries: a Series of Letters* (New York, 1863).

Garraghan, Gilbert J., S.J., *Chapters in Frontier History* (Milwaukee, 1934).

———, *The Jesuits of the Middle United States,* 3 vols. (New York, 1938).

Hodge, Frederick W., ed., *Handbook of American Indians North of Mexico,* 2 vols. (Washington, D. C., 1907).

Magaret, Hélène, *Father De Smet* (New York, 1940). (Well written and trustworthy; a biography in novel form.)

O'Hara, Edwin V., *Pioneer Catholic History of Oregon* (Portland, Ore., 1911).

Parkman, Francis, *The Oregon Trail: Sketches of Prairie and Rocky Mountain Life* (Boston, 1882).

XIII: Orestes Brownson

Brownson, Henry F., *Orestes A. Brownson's Early Life, Middle Life, Later Life,* 3 vols. (Detroit, 1898-1900).

Brownson, Orestes A., *Works,* 20 vols., edited by H. F. Brownson (Detroit, 1882-87).

———, *Selected Essays,* edited by Russell Kirk (Chicago, 1955).

Hecker, Isaac, Five articles on Brownson in the *Catholic World* in 1887.

Maynard, Theodore, *Orestes Brownson: Yankee, Radical, Catholic* (New York, 1943).

Sargent, Daniel, *Four Independents* (New York, 1935). (Contains a long chapter on Brownson, with some excellent comments.)

Schlesinger, Arthur M., Jr., *Orestes Brownson: A Pilgrim's Progress* (Boston, 1939). (Better on the early than on the Catholic years.)

Whalen, Doran, *Granite for God's House* (New York, 1941). (Written by Sister Rose Gertrude Whalen; charming, but often unreliable.)

XIV: Samuel Mazzuchelli

By far the most important item is Mazzuchelli's own *Memoirs* (Chicago, 1915), with an introduction by Archbishop Ireland which rounds out what the writer was too modest to record. More about Mazzuchelli appears in M. M. Hoffmann, *Centennial History of the Archdiocese of Dubuque* (Dubuque, 1938) and John Rothensteiner, *History of the Archdiocese of St. Louis* (St. Louis, 1928), Vol. I, chs. 19-20. An accurate life, in novel form, is Mary Ellen Evans, *The Seed and the Glory* (New York, 1950).

XV: Isaac Hecker

Brownson, Henry F., *Orestes A. Brownson's Early Life, Middle Life, Later Life*, 3 vols. (Detroit, 1898-1900).

Burton, Katherine, *Celestial Homespun* (New York, 1943).

Elliott, Walter, *The Life of Father Hecker* (New York, 1891).

Holden, Vincent F., *The Early Years of Isaac Thomas Hecker* (Washington, D. C., 1939).

Klein, Felix, *Americanism; a Phantom Heresy* (Atchison, Kans., 1951). (Of utmost importance for the treatment of what led up to the papal Letter of 1899.)

McSorley, Joseph, *Father Hecker and His Friends* (St. Louis, 1952).

Maynard, Theodore, *Orestes Brownson* (New York, 1943).

XVI: James Healy

Little has been written about the Healy family. There are short articles in the *Catholic Encyclopedia;* bare notes in such compendiums as those made by Reuss, Corrigan, and Code; a reference in John F. Gillard's *Colored Catholics;* something about them in Sister Mary O'Hanlon's *Heresy of Race* and also in *The History of the Archdiocese of Boston,* by Frs. Lord, Sexton and Harrington. The picture has now been filled in by Fr. Albert S. Foley, S.J.'s *Bishop Healy: Beloved Outcast* (New York, 1954), on which this chapter is chiefly based.

XVII: James Cardinal Gibbons

The Life of James Cardinal Gibbons (2 vols., Milwaukee, 1952) by John Tracy Ellis is a mine of information, although controversial questions are treated with extreme caution. Allen Sinclair Will, whose two-volume biography (New York, 1922) is not as adequate in many ways, presents a more vivid picture of the man himself, whom the author knew personally. Frederick J. Zwierlein's *Life and Letters of Bishop McQuaid* (3 vols., Rochester, 1925-27) and *Letters of Archbishop Corrigan to Bishop McQuaid and Allied Documents* (New York, 1946) unintentionally damage the reputation of the man who was his hero. Other books of importance are Colman J. Barry, *The Catholic Church and the German Americans* (Milwaukee, 1953), James H. Moynihan, *Life of Archbishop Ireland* (New York, 1953), and Stephen Bell, *Rebel, Priest and Prophet: a Biography of Dr. Edward McGlynn* (New York, 1937).

XVIII: Francesca Cabrini

The "official" life, *La Madre Francesca Saverio Cabrini,* written by Sister Xavier de Maria, was published anonymously (Milan, 1928). Two lives appeared in 1945, the year of her canonization: Lucille Papin Borden, *Francesca Cabrini: Without Staff or Scrip,* and Theodore Maynard, *Too Small a World.* A work published by a Benedictine in 1944, *Frances Xavier Cabrini: Saint of Emigrants,* has not been seen.

XIX: Rose Hawthorne Lathrop

The first biography to appear was hurriedly written and not satisfactory, that by James J. Walsh: *Mother Alphonsa* (New York, 1930). The second was the amazingly successful, if often inaccurate, *Sorrow Built a Bridge,* by Katherine Burton (New

York, 1931). My own *A Fire Was Lighted* (Milwaukee, 1948) is based on the many documents put at my disposal by the Sisters at Hawthorne and on some 200 letters in the Houghton Library of Harvard University and the New York Public Library, as well as on other long-available subsidiary material.

XX: Miriam Teresa Demjanovich

The first biography, by Sister M. Zita, a close friend of the subject, was published anonymously (New York, 1936). Odds and ends about her short career are to be found in the *Sister Miriam Teresa League of Prayer Bulletin,* issued at Convent Station, New Jersey. My own biography, *The Better Part* (New York, 1952), was written with the advantage of my being able to utilize statements gathered from those who knew her, and which were intended to initiate her process of beatification.

XXI: Alfred E. Smith

One might feel inclined to say that Governor Smith's autobiography, *Up to Now* (New York, 1929), was studiously restrained—unless one knew the magnanimous and affable nature of the man. *Up from the City Streets* (New York, 1927), by Norman Hapgood and Henry Moskowitz, is a deft piece of writing, and much better than Frank Graham, *Al Smith, American, an Informal Biography* (New York, 1945). Best of all is the account written by his daughter, Emily Smith Warner, in collaboration with Hawthorne Daniel, *The Happy Warrior* (New York, 1956).

DISCARDED
BRENTWOOD PUBLIC LIBRARY